Janice A. Gasker, DSW

"I Never Told Anyone This Before"
Managing the Initial Disclosure of Sexual Abuse Re-Collections

Pre-publication
REVIEW

"**T**his book presents a unique blend of theory, research, and practice guidance on narrative therapy with adult survivors of childhood sexual abuse. The author goes beyond the 'repressed memory' controversy to describe the disclosure of abuse as it is 're-collected' by adults in therapy. A stunning feature of this book is its microanalysis of initial disclosures and the group's silent support. The author discusses the elements needed to create a safe therapeutic environment and offers the practitioner a number of useful strategies for responding appropriately to client disclosure. It addresses the needs of special populations such as sexual and racial minorities."

Roberta G. Sands, PhD
Associate Professor,
University of Pennsylvania
School of Social Work

D1158645

"I Never Told Anyone This Before"
Managing the Initial Disclosure of Sexual Abuse Re-Collections

THE HAWORTH MALTREATMENT AND TRAUMA PRESS
Robert A. Geffner, PhD
Senior Editor

New, Recent, and Forthcoming Titles:

Sexual, Physical, and Emotional Abuse in Out-of-Home Care: Prevention Skills for At-Risk Children by Toni Cavanagh Johnson and Associates

Cedar House: A Model Child Abuse Treatment Program by Bobbi Kendig with Clara Lowry

Bridging Worlds: Understanding and Facilitating Adolescent Recovery from the Trauma of Abuse by Joycee Kennedy and Carol McCarthy

The Learning About Myself (LAMS) Program for At-Risk Parents: Learning from the Past—Changing the Future by Verna Rickard

The Learning About Myself (LAMS) Program for At-Risk Parents: Handbook for Group Participants by Verna Rickard

Treating Children with Sexually Abusive Behavior Problems: Guidelines for Child and Parent Intervention by Jan Ellen Burton, Lucinda A. Rasmussen, Julie Bradshaw, Barbara J. Christopherson, and Steven C. Huke

Bearing Witness: Violence and Collective Responsibility by Sandra L. Bloom and Michael Reichert

Sibling Abuse Trauma: Assessment and Intervention Strategies for Children, Families, and Adults by John V. Caffaro and Allison Conn-Caffaro

From Surviving to Thriving: A Therapist's Guide to Stage II Recovery for Survivors of Childhood Abuse by Mary Bratton

"I Never Told Anyone This Before": Managing the Initial Disclosure of Sexual Abuse Re-Collections by Janice A. Gasker

Breaking the Silence: Group Therapy for Childhood Sexual Abuse, A Practitioner's Manual by Judith A. Margolin

Stopping the Violence: A Group Model to Change Men's Abusive Attitudes and Behaviors by David J. Decker

Stopping the Violence: A Group Model to Change Men's Abusive Attitudes and Behaviors—The Client Workbook by David J. Decker

"I Never Told Anyone This Before"
Managing the Initial Disclosure of Sexual Abuse Re-Collections

Janice A. Gasker, DSW

HMTP

The Haworth Maltreatment and Trauma Press
An Imprint of The Haworth Press, Inc.
New York • London

Published by

The Haworth Maltreatment and Trauma Press, an imprint of The Haworth Press, Inc., 10 Alice Street, Binghamton, NY 13904-1580

Cover design by Marylouise E. Doyle.

The Library of Congress has cataloged the hardcover edition of this book as:

Gasker, Janice A.
    I never told anyone this before : managing the initial disclosure of sexual abuse re-collections/ Janice A. Gasker.
        p.   cm.
    Includes bibliographical references and index.
    ISBN 0-7890-0461-5 (alk. paper)
    1. Sexual abuse victims—Treatment. 2. Sexual abuse victims—Medical care. 3. Psychother-apy. I. Title.
RC560.S44G37 1999
616.85′83690651—dc21   98-39342
                                                                                                                            CIP

ISBN 0-7890-0462-3 (pbk.)

CONTENTS

20.48

99462

ABOUT THE AUTHOR

Janice Gasker, DSW, ACSW, LSW, has worked with persons surviving sexual abuse for over twelve years. She currently has a private psychotherapy and human service agency consultation practice in Lehigh Valley, Pennsylvania. Dr. Gasker has taught clinical practice and social science research at the University of Pennsylvania School of Social Work, Widener University Center for Social Work Education, West Chester University, and Marywood College Graduate School of Social Work. She is a member of the Academy of Certified Social Workers and the National Association of Social Workers. Currently, she is Assistant Professor of Social Work at Kutztown University of Pennsylvania.

Acknowledgments

This book is a result of my relationships with many people. I would like to take this opportunity to thank a few of them. Thanks to The Haworth Press and Robert Geffner, editor, for being willing to take on this difficult and controversial issue.

I am indebted to Roberta Sands, PhD, and Frederick Erickson, PhD, of the University of Pennsylvania for their support and guidance of the seminal research. Thanks also to the entire faculty of the University of Pennsylvania School of Social Work for caring so much about the quality of the learning experience there. I would like to especially thank my current colleagues at Kutztown University for providing a rare work environment that is at once challenging, stimulating, and supportive.

I am also grateful for having had the opportunity to know and work with the many clinicians and clients who have helped me to understand the therapeutic process. Most important in this group is the therapist whose work is analyzed here. She was willing to allow her work to be minutely scrutinized purely for the sake of professional knowledge. As is evident in the chapters that follow, she is an outstanding clinician; she is also an extraordinary person. Her clients, family, and friends are indeed fortunate to have her presence in their life stories. She must remain anonymous here, but she has my deepest gratitude.

I would like to thank the women in my life whose friendship makes all of my work possible, especially Toni, Pat, Sue, Fenna, Cindy, and Lisa. Finally, I would like to acknowledge members of my family, many of whom are relatives by circumstance, but friends by choice. Special thanks to my husband Sherrod, whose support and understanding go with me in all my endeavors. And loving thanks to my daughter Alice, for telling her first-grade teacher that her favorite authors are "Dr. Seuss and my mom."

Introduction

A PSYCHOTHERAPIST'S DILEMMA

Childhood sexual abuse has come to be an American household word. Discussions about incest and the molestation of children have progressed from whispers behind closed doors to shouting matches on national television. Along with escalating concern about the issue, increasing numbers of people concerned about their own childhood histories are seeking help. Unfortunately, it is difficult to determine the most effective means of providing help in an atmosphere charged with emotionality and controversy. To make matters still more challenging for the mental health practitioner, this controversy permeates the scientific literature as well as mainstream society.

Painful Memories Sought Out

Many members of mainstream American society find the notion of child sexual abuse, particularly incest, so abhorrent as to be unthinkable. (For a discussion of the development of this view, see, for example, Bremner, 1971; Costin, 1985; Gardner, 1992a, 1992b; and Zelizer, 1985.) This feeling has become part of a professional perspective that child sexual abuse may be so unthinkable that it can be repressed for years, even decades, and then finally recalled in adulthood, often as part of a therapeutic process aimed at seeking out the causes of current psychosocial disturbances (Goldstein and Farmer, 1992, 1993; Lawrence, 1993; Tavris, 1993).

Traumatic Memories Found

The therapeutic goal for survivors of childhood trauma is always to recover and to heal. Unfortunately, the means to that end is not clear-cut. For example, some writers have suggested that the process of seeking out traumatic memories, to identify them clearly as a means of recovering from the experience, is both ineffective and detrimental (Furer, 1993; Gavigan-Reno, 1993; Goldstein and Farmer, 1992; Wakefield and Underwager, 1988). These sources suggest that certain therapeutic approaches may result in clients developing memories of childhood sexual abuse that are not based on historical events, and that these memories are deleterious to functioning.

The relationship between repressed memory and adult re-collections of childhood sexual abuse has been framed as a true-or-false debate . . .

To Believe or Not To Believe

The controversy has come to a head with adults who come to bear re-collections of childhood sexual abuse. The relationship between repressed memory and adult re-collections of childhood sexual abuse has been framed as a true-or-false debate in both the popular and scientific media.

On one hand, adults who come to bear memories of childhood sexual abuse are thought to be the helpless victims of incest who are only further damaged by mental health professionals and others who doubt the credibility of their reports (Berliner, 1993; Freyd, 1993; Lawrence, 1993; Maltz, 1990; Maltz and Holman, 1987). It is believed that the process of questioning reporters' credibility may not only harm them but may result in a return to the days when men, women, and children who reported sexual mistreatment were disbelieved as a matter of course.

The other side of the argument also sees the reporters as victims, not of sexual abuse, but of misguided, overzealous therapists who in their zeal to ferret out memories of childhood trauma succeed only in suggesting it (see, for example, Ganaway, 1993; Gardner, 1992b; Goldstein and Farmer, 1992; Lief, 1992; Perry, 1993). Therapists are viewed as implanting memories that are revisited in the therapeutic process in excruciating detail, leaving the bearer of the memories with the same degree of trauma as if the abuse had actually occurred.

The current controversy highlights the possibility that persons may be harmed rather than helped in the therapeutic process.

To the helping professional, the debate may be confusing and disconcerting. Faced with the prospect of working with a possible survivor of childhood sexual abuse, clinicians may be unsure about the therapeutic approach to take. The current controversy highlights the possibility that persons may be harmed rather than helped in the therapeutic process.

New guidelines are being developed as an outcome of thoughtful research. These guidelines are being created by and for therapists who specialize in work with adults who bear memories of sexual trauma. Suggestions are being offered regarding therapeutic goals, general information, and the processing of traumatic memories (see, for example, Phelps, Friedlander, and Enns, 1997; Waites, 1997). What even the newest research lacks, however, is a focus on the very genesis of this therapeutic challenge. Until now, there has not been a close examination of the way clients begin to speak about their abuse histories and how the therapist might facilitate that all-important initial disclosure without influencing the unfolding of the story. For the clinical generalist and the beginning practitioner, many pressing questions remain.

Even the newest research is lacking a focus on the way clients begin to speak about their abuse histories . . . about how the therapist might facilitate that initial disclosure without influencing the unfolding of the story.

For example: Should a client who reports the sudden realization that he or she has been abused as a child be believed as a matter of course? Or should the therapist attempt to verify the allegation before proceeding with the development of a treatment plan? Should the helping professional seek out potentially traumatizing childhood memories? Or should he or she avoid discussing them for fear of creating them? Is the truth or falsity of such reports even relevant to treatment?

These uncertainties are compounded by the fact that people who bear memories of childhood sexual abuse are suffering extreme emotional pain. Perhaps the suffering is due to unresolved memories of real events, and then again, perhaps it is due to misguided

perceptions of events that did not occur. In the meantime, consequences of the debate are being felt by clients, mental health professionals, and the family members of persons who come to believe
they have been victims.

A More Relevant Question

It is the responsibility of mental health practitioners to develop
guidelines for practice based on systematic inquiry into the phenomenon. Although the debate within the therapeutic community
threatens the unity and credibility of all helping professions, the
problem is not limited to the so-called "false memory" controversy.

---

*For helping professionals, the question most in need of an answer
is:* **How might we use our clients' memories of traumatic events
to enhance the quality of their lives?**

To answer this question, it is necessary to put together what is
already known about human memory and the way it affects persons' lives. A fresh look at the way re-collected traumatic memory
influences the life of the memory bearer is necessary. In addition, a
significant part of the answer lies in a careful inspection of the way
reports of traumatic childhood events emerge in the helping process
and the role of the helper in the context of their evolution. This is
the crucial initial disclosure that provides the focal point of this
book.

---

*A significant part of the answer lies in a careful inspection of the way
reports of traumatic childhood events emerge in the helping process
and the role of the helper in the context of their evolution.*

Note that the historical accuracy of traumatic memories is all but
irrelevant here. The focus is holistic. It simply seeks to answer the
question of what is to be done by the therapist in the best interests of
his or her clients.

Although the question of historical accuracy may be directly relevant to the client's best interests in some cases, in others, this consideration is at most peripheral. For the participants of the research that supports this book, questions of historical accuracy played a very minor role. Likewise, the investigation of the truthfulness of abuse reports is notably absent here. On the other hand, the potential for changes in re-collections during the therapeutic process is an important consideration in the chapters that follow.

Chapter 1 constructs a theoretical foundation for the discussion of memory in the therapeutic setting. Chapter 2 provides a vocabulary for discussing adult memories of childhood sexual abuse that empowers the memory bearer and is consistent with the most current empirical knowledge. Chapter 3 presents an innovative conceptualization of the process through which re-collections of sexual abuse are brought into consciousness, shared with others, and eventually shaped into integral parts of the life story.

Chapter 4 focuses on the initial disclosure of abuse within the structure of the therapeutic setting. Chapter 5 is an even closer look at the first-time telling of abuse stories, focusing on the verbal and non-verbal cues that make up the social environment of the disclosure.

The final four chapters provide specific therapeutic guidelines. Chapter 6 is a discussion of the therapeutic implications of the view of sexual abuse disclosures as life narratives. Three basic foundations for practice that grow out of this perspective are discussed. Chapter 7 gives concrete practice guidelines and therapeutic techniques. These facilitate a therapy environment conducive to disclosures of sexual abuse re-collections in a manner that both beneficial to the client and protective of the therapist's professional integrity. Chapter 8 offers unique techniques and considerations for work with special populations, and Chapter 9 contains troubleshooting guidelines for work with particularly challenging situations. Taken together, these final chapters provide a clear perspective as well as specific techniques for facilitating the initial disclosure of childhood sexual abuse re-collections in a planned, therapeutic way.

An appendix discusses the research methods employed in the study of disclosures of sexual abuse in the clinical setting. It concludes with ethical caveats related to research of this type.

THEORETICAL ISSUES

Chapter 1

Moving Beyond the Debate: Theoretical Perspectives

The controversy regarding adults who come to bear memories of childhood abuse centers around fundamental beliefs about the nature of the human memory of experience. The issue at hand in the current literature is whether brand-new memories of old trauma may be historically accurate recollections of real events or simply *re-collections,* that is, images that are pieced together which come to be part of our self-constructed life stories.

This chapter lends a theoretical foundation to the discussion of adult re-collection of childhood sexual abuse, considering the phenomenon from a variety of perspectives, including psychoanalytic, developmental, and cognitive theories of psychology, folkloristic studies, and the sociology of knowledge. This demonstrates the variety of lenses through which the subject can be understood and begins a preliminary identification of issues relevant to social work practice and research.

PSYCHOANALYTIC DRIVE THEORY

The belief that traumatic memories are accurate representations of objective reality that may exist unchanged outside of consciousness is as old as the systematic study of psychiatry.

Freud's earliest work, on the seduction theory, in which he postulated that emotional disturbance is the result of repressed childhood trauma, had this belief as its foundation. Freud later moved from seduction theory to drive theory, which holds that statements regarding childhood sexual abuse may be the result of id-driven fantasy. Due to this change in focus from memories of trauma to memories of fantasy, it is common for Freud to be blamed for the decades-long disbelief of women and children who reported sexual mistreatment (Masson, 1984).

The belief that traumatic memories are accurate representations of objective reality that may exist outside of consciousness is as old as the systematic study of psychiatry.

Screen Memories

Regardless of whether drive theory is consistent with the idea that child sexual abuse exists, Freud's real contribution to the question of the accuracy of traumatic memories lies in his work on the concealing of memories from early childhood. In his essay on this topic, written in 1899, Freud suggested that although childhood memories might be inaccurate due to the child's perceptions of actual traumatic life events, the accurate memory may be intact. That is, accurate memories may be stored and hidden by concealing, or screen, memories. For example, a screen memory might take the form of a large, black spider in a room where a traumatic event took place.

This screen memory provides a block for another memory of the actual trauma. These traumatic memories are viewed as historically accurate and retrievable in psychoanalysis (Freud, 1938).

Freud used convincing case studies as well as introspective autobiographical accounts to support his views. This work could be used to support the generalized acceptance of traumatic memories as historically accurate, particularly those that have grown out of the helping process. Although many of Freud's ideas have been subjected to modern empirical study, his notions about memory have not been systematically evaluated (Fisher and Greenberg, 1985).

Dissociation

Freud was not the first to address the subject of traumatic event memory. Freud's work is based on that of his predecessor, Pierre Janet (Van der Kolk and Van der Hart, 1991).

As early as 1886, Janet documented—based on case studies—that traumatic event memory could exist intact, outside of consciousness. Although the concepts of dissociation and repression are frequently used interchangeably, both ideas are rooted in Janet's work on dissociation. As a defense mechanism, the concept of dissociation refers specifically to unconscious material stored in a way that renders other material inaccessible.

Although Freud was unclear about how repressed material is stored out of consciousness, Janet viewed dissociated material as maintained in a specific way along with a specific affect, that is, the affect that was generated at the time of the trauma. He postulated that the affective content of the dissociated material determines the accessibility of the information. Thus, dissociated material stored in the brain under extreme stress is inextricably linked with that emotion. The dissociated memory may be retrieved only under the same stress level that was present when the trauma was experienced (Spiegel, 1990).

Pierre Janet: Traumatic Memory

Janet distinguished narrative memory from traumatic memory, defining the latter as the automatic integration of new information without much conscious attention to what is happening. Janet believed that humans have this automatic synthesizing of traumatic memory in common with animals, while he viewed narrative memory as uniquely human.

For Janet, traumatic memory could exist in a fixed, inflexible way outside of consciousness. This memory could hinder functioning, as it was evoked under particular conditions.

One case study that supported this theory involved a woman who did not consciously remember her mother's death but acted out the traumatic incident repeatedly and with unvarying detail when under stress (Van der Kolk and Van der Hart, 1991).

Van der Kolk and Van der Hart (1991) have postulated that animal research revealing physiological changes under conditions of stress supports Janet's original theory. They have concluded that a subject may maintain a traumatic memory outside of consciousness, but reexperience it in other environmentally or emotionally similar situations. This model describes the processing of trauma as a dissociation from consciousness, a widely accepted theory employed in the treatment of a wide range of trauma victims and those who suffer from the set of symptoms known as post-traumatic stress disorder (Brom, Kleber, and Witzum, 1992; Classen, Koopman, and Spiegel, 1993; Kluft, 1992; Young, 1992).

The traumatic memory may be maintained outside of consciousness but reexperienced under environmentally or emotionally similar circumstances.

The Therapeutic Quest for Traumatic Memories

The work of Janet and those who followed him—most particularly Freud—began a new perspective on the therapeutic use of memory. Traumatic childhood memories came to be viewed as the cause of many emotional disturbances. For this reason, the memories had to be sought out. Such techniques as hypnosis, dream analysis, and free association were developed as part of psychoanalysis specifically for shedding light on memories hidden in the unconscious (Fisher and Greenberg, 1985).

A comprehensive review of the literature (Tillman, Nash, and Lerner, 1996) has suggested that most contemporary theories regarding trauma and its treatment have adopted similar models in which a goal of treatment is the uncovering of traumatic memories. It should be noted that theories which explain information processing are generally cognitive in their orientation; however, the majority of those regarding trauma assume the psychoanalytic constructs of repression and dissociation (e.g., Burgess and Hartman, 1988).

Traditional psychoanalytic theory, then, suggests that memory of traumatic events may be historically accurate. The trauma may be dissociated or repressed when it occurs and retrieved later in life— particularly while undergoing psychoanalysis. This way of thinking appears to be the foundation for the polarization of the debate regarding the historical accuracy of adult re-collection of childhood sexual abuse.

Theoretical Effects

Miller's (1983) work on memories of childhood maltreatment and their effects on adult functioning is an expression of the sense of urgency that has characterized the debate about adult re-collections of childhood sexual abuse. Miller's work is based on years of practicing psychoanalysis as well as research on the psychohistory of various well-known personalities, from Adolf Hitler to Sylvia Plath. Her work suggests that to some degree all members of today's society have been victims of child abuse, or "poisonous pedagogy" (p. xii). Poisonous pedagogy is a term describing the physical, sexual, or emotional maltreatment of children, which is followed by a denial of the negative emotions that result from the maltreatment. That is, they are taught to be unaware of what is happening to them. These circumstances result in the following individual stages that Miller postulates are common to the lives of most people:

1. To be hurt as a small child without anyone recognizing the situation as such.
2. To fail to react to the resulting suffering with anger.
3. To show gratitude for what are supposed to be good intentions.
4. To forget everything.
5. To discharge the stored-up anger onto others in adulthood or to direct it against oneself. (p. 106)

For Miller, it is imperative that people come to remember their childhood experiences and the negative emotions attached to them to avoid unconsciously passing them on to the next generation in a never-ending cycle. To come in contact with these memories of maltreatment, mistreated children must have contact with at least one person who will believe them. It is essential that this person understand that no blame should be placed on the child; this approach "can be instrumental in either saving or destroying a life" (1983, p. 284).

Psychodynamic Treatment Implications

Miller's work articulates an urgent concern regarding the treatment of adults who come to bear re-collections of childhood sexual abuse. Victims must locate some person who will hear their stories and believe them. This view, however, is not completely representative of the psychoanalytic perspective.

Historical Accuracy of Traumatic Memories

From the earliest days of systematic inquiry, the historical accuracy of memory has not been the focus of theoreticians. Janet provided the foundation for the concept of the dissociation of traumatic memory, but he also wrote, "It is not necessary that the carriage wheel should really have passed over the patient; it is enough if he has the idea that the wheel passed over his legs" (Janet, 1907, p. 324).

From the earliest days of systematic inquiry, the historical accuracy of memory has not been the focus.

Likewise, dissociation, in Sullivan's object-relations theory, was a functionally distinct subset of personality created as a defense against anxiety created by general themes—*not specific events*—in early relationships (Newman, 1990).

Another theory of object relations (McDougall, 1985) uses theater as a metaphor for psychic reality in which the scriptwriter is a childlike *I* struggling in an adult world. Following this theater metaphor, perceptions of events are fit into old dramas; that is, memories are fit into the plots that already exist. Internalized mental representations, which include both word representatives and affect representatives, are interpretations of experience. These mental representations are not historically accurate records. Similar to Sullivan's explanation of dissociation, McDougall (1985) described unconscious, intrapsychic representations as generalized scenarios, not specific memories of single events. In times of stress, these scenarios may "shift from one stage to another," due to the flexibility of the individual character (p. 4).

Finally, Freud explored the idea that particular childhood memories may be related in a symbolic fashion during the psychoanalytic process, making the narrative choices in relating them grist for the analytic mill:

the so-called earliest childhood recollections are not true memory traces but later elaborations of the same, elaborations which might have been subjected to the influences of many later psychic forces. (Freud, 1938, p. 65)

Memory, or narrative truth, is a construction that is formulated and reformulated over time . . .

Memory As Functional

Relating memories in a certain way for a certain purpose in the psychoanalytic setting has captured the attention of Spence (1982) and others (e.g., Hedges, 1994; Schafer, 1976). Spence (1982) has conceptualized *narrative truth* as the construction of meaning and memory in the therapeutic interaction. Spence wrote that memory, or narrative truth, is a construction that is formulated and reformulated over time:

> the criterion we use to decide when a certain experience has been captured to our satisfaction . . . depends on continuity and closure and the extent to which the fit of the pieces takes on an aesthetic finality. (p. 31)

Spence contrasts narrative truth with historical truth, that which has to do with relating an objective occurrence.

In the psychodynamic view, then, memory is functional. The focus of concern is its role in the present. Historical accuracy has not been a significant issue.

COGNITIVE PSYCHOLOGICAL THEORY

Cognitive psychological theory has suggested a perspective on adult re-collections of childhood sexual abuse that at first blush seems directly opposed to that proposed by psychoanalytic theory. In fact, however, there appear to be more similarities than differences. A general cognitive model will be reviewed here first, to provide a beginning point.

> *There is empirical support in the field of cognitive psychology for concluding that the potential exists for the development of memories that do not correspond to historical events.*

The Good Strategy Use Model

The Good Strategy Use Model (Schneider and Pressley, 1989) is presented here due to its holistic, metatheoretical look at the psychological and physiological aspects of memory. As a traditional cognitive theory, its focus is on the individual and the individual's means of processing information. This model highlights three basic requirements for recall: (1) strategies, the coordinated development and use of strategies for remembering such as imagery, summarizing, and rehearsal; (2) metacognition, the knowledge about one's own memory capabilities; and (3) nonstrategic knowledge base, a context for information. This model is based on the synthesis of large numbers of experiments on the memory capabilities of children ages two through twenty. It accounts for a broad range of memory functions, including the memorization of facts and storage of information about environmental stimuli as well as the retention of accounts of experience (albeit not traumatic event memory per se); however, it does not address the neurophysiological mechanisms involved in the memory process. It is especially relevant here in that it emphasizes the integration of strategies, metacognition, and knowledge (or beliefs) about one's own ability to recall events. Because they all play a role, this model suggests a reconstruction of memory as it is recalled. In other words, it implies that memory may be a construction, as opposed to a video-type recording of historical perception.

From this perspective, autobiographical memory, as it is held as belief, is the person's creation. Moreover, it is the creation of a person in concert with the social milieu.

There is both empirical and anecdotal support in the field of cognitive psychology for concluding that the potential exists for the development of images perceived to be memories that do not correspond to historical events (Furer, 1993; Gavigan-Reno, 1993; Goldstein and Farmer, 1993; Loftus and Davies, 1984; Loftus and Fathi, 1985; Loftus and Greene, 1980; Loftus and Loftus, 1980).

Memory can be seen as an active organization of past experiences in which past and present are combined and shuffled to meet current needs.

Memory As Active Information Processing

Bartlett's (1932) classic work on memory is an example. One of the first comprehensive works in the field of cognitive science, the book is based on laboratory studies conducted with large numbers of educated adults in London during World War I. Bartlett asked his subjects to perform a number of tasks related to perception, imagery, and recall. His findings suggested that as events occur a static "trace" is not created in the brain. Rather, the past seems to operate as an organized mass. Elaborating on the then-new concept of "schema," Bartlett called this type of organization an *active* organization of past experiences in which present and past are combined and shuffled to meet current needs. To explain this cognitive process, he suggested that persons follow a course of memory development related to their surroundings and their self-images: "This and this and this must have occurred, in order that my present state should be what it is" (p. 202). Bartlett's work represents a thread in the development of cognitive science, which for a time had been lost but has recently been retrieved—the link between an individual's social environment and information processing.

Memory As "Misinformation"

The work of Elizabeth Loftus is most often cited as an example of a method of examining the way in which memory of events is an individual and social production. Loftus has coined the phrase "misinformation effect" and has demonstrated the effect of suggestion on the accuracy of certain types of memory.

Loftus has presented anecdotal evidence that supports the potential for implanting a traumatic memory (of being lost in a mall as a child). The "misinformation," a memory of being lost, came to be believed by both adolescent and adult subjects based on manipulative suggestions by a researcher and the corroboration of a family member (Loftus, 1993). While such reports do not demonstrate that new memories of past childhood sexual abuse are false, they do lend support to the notion that some memories are the product of both individual and social factors. Although these may be perceived as personal experiences, they may not correspond to historical events.

Campbell Perry, a cognitively oriented professor of psychiatry at Concordia University, made a conference presentation that included the anecdote of a famous occurrence of the implantation of a memory—the "kidnapping" of Jean Piaget. Perry (1993) said:

> We have the testament of Jean Piaget, the noted Swiss psychologist, of an early memory of about age two of an attempt to kidnap him in his pram. Almost thirteen years later when he was fifteen, his former nanny wrote a letter to his parents saying that she had contrived the whole incident and returned the watch she had received for her presumed valor on that occasion. But what's interesting is that Piaget writes, years later, that he can still visualize the whole set of events, even though he knows that they are wrong and that they didn't happen and the whole thing was fabricated by the nanny and that it was probably the result of his parents talking about it over the years . . .

Therapists might doubt the validity of reports of traumatic incidents, potentially jeopardizing the helping relationship . . .

"False" Memories?

Current literature in cognitive science clearly supports the potential for the development of historically inaccurate memories. Therapeutic implications that have grown from this perspective include the use of psychoeducational and present-oriented techniques geared toward altering dysfunctional beliefs (e.g., Jehu, Klassen, and Gazan, 1985). However, another clinical implication is that therapists might doubt the validity of their clients' reports of traumatic incidents. This doubt might jeopardize the helping relationship, leaving clients without professional assistance in managing a most difficult emotional situation.

For therapeutic purposes, the truth or falsity of an individual's memory of a traumatic event has not been a central focus. The objective accuracy of memory is seldom viewed as significant to the helping process.

Similar to psychodynamic theorists, leaders in the field of cognitive psychology do not rule out the potential for the sudden appearance of historically accurate memories. Most interventions—even those based on cognitive theory—with persons identified as sexual abuse survivors include a focus on memories of the traumatic event (Haugaard and Reppucci, 1988).

The degree of focus on the memories of traumatic events varies, as does the assumption that these memories are historically accurate. What is clear is the division between those who choose to question the validity of such memories and those who choose not to do so.

FOLKLORISTIC STUDIES

In an effort to get beyond this division, research regarding adult re-collections of childhood sexual abuse from the field of folklore is reviewed here. This discipline provides a different perspective. Interestingly, however, this perspective also yields what appears to be a polarized view.

On one hand, the study of folklore reveals beliefs in such phenomena as satanic ritual abuse (often linked to adult re-collections of childhood sexual abuse) as socially produced urban myths. Victors (1993) has studied beliefs regarding incidents and experiences of satanic ritual abuse. In a comprehensive study of regions in which such reports were openly discussed and reported in local newspapers, he concluded that there was no historically accurate basis for the beliefs. In other words, he could find no evidence that satanic cults were operating in the area. He tied the beliefs in ritual abuse to general societal unrest and suggested that although such beliefs may be held by individuals (and consequently believed to be personal experiences) they were in fact socially produced. Not one individual's experience of satanic ritual abuse was necessary to create a community's belief in the event. Similar interpretations have been made regarding beliefs in supernatural experiences.

Not one individual's experience of satanic ritual abuse was necessary to create a community's belief in the event.

Regarding adult re-collections of childhood sexual abuse, it has been suggested that satanic ritual abuse myths, New Age thought, feminism, "recovery" therapy, and the media have influenced the development of such beliefs (Goldstein and Farmer, 1992). The perspective of the urban myth has the benefit of highlighting the powerful impact of the community. Such folkloristic studies suggest that consideration of social phenomena is a necessary component of any systematic inquiry into adult re-collections of childhood sexual abuse. Of course, an exclusive focus on the role played by social dimensions in the exploration of this phenomenon could result in a suppression of the voice of the bearers of the memories and a misrepresentation of their individual experiences.

An exclusive focus on the role played by social dimensions could result in a suppression of the voice of the bearers of the memories and a misrepresentation of their individual experiences.

Folklorists sometimes study the stories people tell about themselves in a manner grounded in reports of individual experience. Hufford (1982, 1993) has developed an experiential theory from such a perspective. This theory explains beliefs and legends about supernatural events. It explores beliefs as they are held by individuals about themselves in a manner that to the greatest extent possible respects the integrity of reporters.

As a result, this perspective demands the exploration of the possibility that an historically accurate traumatic experience has actually occurred. Individual perceptions are of paramount interest. It is assumed that some type of traumatic event is behind every belief in a traumatic event. Whether the report is exactly accurate in all details is of little interest; there is an avoidance of attempts to determine the historical accuracy or inaccuracy of the beliefs. It is more important to note each individual's perceptions of events. In fact, adults who have come to bear memories of childhood sexual abuse have reported experiences remarkably similar to those reported by Hufford's subjects, who believed themselves to be victims of supernatural assault (Gasker, 1993).

This theory highlights the possibility that an historically accurate memory of some type of trauma intersects with the development of a belief that childhood sexual abuse has occurred. This consideration of persons' perceived experiences also must be part of any inquiry into the "truth" of adult re-collections of childhood sexual abuse.

SOCIOLOGY OF KNOWLEDGE

The beginnings of a reconciliation between perspectives that view beliefs as socially produced and those which view beliefs as individually produced may be found in the sociology of knowledge. Berger and Luckmann's (1967) treatment of the sociology of knowledge provides a vehicle for viewing knowledge as socially constructed, yet experienced by the individual.

Persons together communicate and evolve a determination of what is real, what experiences have occurred, and what these mean to their lives.

This analysis of the process of the construction of belief suggests a dynamic society of individuals interacting and shaping one anothers' beliefs. It includes consideration of phenomena that seem to be independent of one's apprehension. This perception leads to the intersubjective nature of reality in which persons interact and communicate to negotiate what is real. For example, if reality becomes problematic as perceived, the perceiver seeks to incorporate it into his or her current conceptualization of reality through interaction with others. The means of conducting this interaction is language, by which "non-everyday experiences" are translated into the "paramount reality of everyday life" (Berger and Luckmann, 1967,

p. 26). This conversational interaction provides an ongoing modification of reality as it is expressed by individuals:

> At the same time that the conversational apparatus continuously maintains reality, it continuously modifies it. Items are dropped and added, weakening some sectors of what is still being taken for granted and reinforcing others. Thus, the subjective reality of something that is never talked about comes to be shaky. (p. 153)

Thus, persons together communicate and evolve a determination of what is real, what experiences have occurred, and what these mean to their lives.

For this theory, language objectifies experience. Recent findings of researchers in the field of sociolinguistics indicate that communication is a collaborative phenomenon and consequently support this theory (Kendon, 1990).

Truth As Improvisation

Truth is an elusive concept at all times. It is most particularly so in light of the phenomenon of adult re-collections of childhood sexual abuse. For psychoanalytic theory, traumatic memories are perhaps historically accurate, but need to be interpreted in the context of the telling. Cognitive psychology clearly demonstrates the potential for the development of very real memories that are not historically accurate, but that represent the product of dynamic mental processes. Folklore studies point simultaneously to the importance of the individual as well as the collective experience in the development of memory and belief. The sociology of knowledge suggests that what is true is based in individual perceptions only as those are interpreted in a dynamic, meaning-making society.

Memory and meaning-making are not independent phenomena. Each occurs in the intersection of the individual and the environment.

The Importance of the Telling

Interaction is the common thread. Each of the perspectives reviewed recognizes that memory and meaning-making are not independent phenomena; each occurs in the intersection of the individual and the immediate environment. Viewed in this context, the concept of collaborative meaning-making holds promise for the question of what is "truth" in light of adult re-collections of sexual abuse. The perspective that communication is a collaborative phenomenon has been explored by Fogel (1993) in the field of developmental psychology. Here, a cognitive and developmental orientation have been combined with an interactional perspective—Bartlett's concept revisited.

Information in the Context of Relationship

Fogel's (1993) ideas about memory and interactional communication have led to the concept of *embodied cognition*. Embodied cognition refers to cognitive aspects of relationships. Based on empirically grounded assertions regarding developmental changes in communication as well as the philosophy of Vico,* the concept of embodied cognition acknowledges that a central feature of relationships is the creation of information through perception and cognition. Cognition is conceptualized as:

> . . . embodied and relational, a reflection of our participation in a dynamic perception-action system, not a record of objective or represented contents of "reality." (Fogel, 1993, p. 120)

This dynamic system model has also yielded two concepts directly related to memory: participatory cognition, in which prior experience automatically is brought to bear on current action, and imaginative cognition, which has the perceived purpose of remembering something that has been done, seen, felt, or heard (Fogel, 1993).

---

*Giambattista Vico was one of the new Italian modernists of the latter part of the seventeenth century who wrote on the unification of the sciences and knowledge and the subjectivity of truth, against such philosophers as Descartes. He is perhaps best known for his belief that *verum* (truth), and *factum* (made), are one and the same (Palmer, 1988).

Participatory cognition, then, is similar to unconscious cognition. Some past experiences are not part of current awareness, although they may influence current behavior. On the other hand, imaginative cognition is similar to consciousness. This type of cognition is conceptualized as perceptions of prior events that are brought into awareness for a purpose—the purpose of relating those events to and with others. Fogel (1993) wrote, "the remembered past is co-regulated with respect to the present situation and appears as a meaningful present experience in relation to that situation" (p. 126). For Fogel, memory is a continuous process.

The truth of a memory has to do with its purpose in the present context.

Memory: A Functional Process

This view of memory is useful in the context of the exploration of objectivity in adult re-collections of childhood sexual abuse for several reasons. It recognizes the role of both the individual perception and collective experience in creating memory. In this way, neither the social influence nor the individual voice is suppressed. In addition, the function of any re-collection becomes its own truth in the moment.

Truth is negotiated between the individual holding the perception of trauma and the individuals in the very active role of listener.

In other words, the truth of a memory has to do with its purpose in the present context. Truth is negotiated between the individual holding the perception of trauma and any individuals playing the very active role of listener in the interaction.

Relative Truth

Bruner (1986) has suggested that truth is what is right in its own world and that there are many possible worlds. Based on the philosophy of Nelson Goodman, emphasizing the constructivism of reality ("world" is created by "mind") as well as empirical studies in cognitive and developmental psychology, Bruner's work—similar to Fogel's—describes truth as negotiated in the present among participants.

This is not to suggest viewing the phenomenon of adult re-collections of childhood sexual abuse under the diffuse light of absolute relativism. Rather, it is to suggest that the concepts of collaborative meaning-making and constructivism be applied to the discussion. Bruner (1990) has melded the fields of cognitive science and literary analysis to provide the foundations of a narrative psychology in which he suggests that the process of human meaning-making is central to any study of behavior. He has suggested that a perspective that includes consideration of collaborative meaning-making and constructivism of memory need not result in inescapable relativism:

> Constructivism's basic claim is simply that knowledge is "right" or "wrong" in light of the perspective we have chosen to assume. Rights and wrongs of this kind—however well we can test them—do not sum to absolute truths and falsities. The best we can hope for is that we be aware of our own perspective and those of others when we make our claims of "rightness" and "wrongness." (p. 25)

Right and wrong, true and false—all are relative concepts that have meaning specific to the situations created by individuals.

The truth is in the telling and its social context.

The Truth Is in the Telling

Ultimately, the truth is in the telling and its social context. This perspective has relevance for inquiry into adult re-collections of childhood sexual abuse in a number of ways. First, it is a way of allowing structured inquiry without suppressing client perceptions in favor of historical events. Second, it is consistent with humanistic values in that it views memory holders as active agents in the creation of their own life stories who have the potential to be more consciously powerful social agents in the creation of the shared development of truths. Finally, it recognizes the inherent impact of re-collection on the here-and-now experience of clients: "Memories are active experiences in the present and they mean something different each time they are remembered" (Fogel, 1993, p. 127). This highlights the potential impact of the use of re-collection in the therapeutic process as a powerful, dynamic force that shapes emotions and behaviors.

A close look is needed at the way clients share life stories about childhood sexual abuse and the context in which they are shared.

FIRST-TIME TELLING

This review demonstrates the importance of memory in therapy and the relative insignificance of its historical accuracy to the therapeutic endeavor. The therapeutic power of re-collection is unquestionable. Clearly, it is important for the helping process to facilitate the telling of traumatic stories. But the storytelling process itself remains ambiguous. The exact therapeutic techniques that foster the first-time telling of a sexual abuse re-collection and its subsequent revision remain unclear. A close look is needed at the way clients share life stories about childhood sexual abuse and the context in which they are shared.

Chapter 2

Revisionist Vocabulary

Everything about memories of childhood sexual abuse is currently controversial. In our society, the terms used to describe concepts related to these memories carry heavy emotional baggage. Once it may have been perfectly fine to make diagnostic note of a fugue state, but those days are gone. A worker cannot speak of a client with memory lapses without calling up images of multiple personality disorder, "false memory syndrome," Sybil, and a host of conflicting—and frequently negative—connotations. These connotations are part of popular culture and are part of the life experience of clients as well as workers. They color thinking and influence behavior.

It is imperative that professionals step away from these popular conceptualizations and get back to basic science. Basic science is a systematic observation of events. Here terms and definitions will be created that are based on empirical study of the phenomenon of the disclosure of memories of childhood sexual abuse. The concepts and terms have been designed to avoid to the extent possible any emotional influence from popular culture.

In addition to providing a scientific foundation, it is imperative that therapists and researchers present a client-friendly voice. In the societal discourse on this subject, professionals must speak in a manner that helps clients' voices to be respected and heard. Therefore, there is a dual objective in creating this new language. The revisionist vocabulary must accomplish two things: first, it must reflect the current state of empirical knowledge; second, it must be radically client centered.

This is a radically different perspective from one that assumes there is an objective reality that a client may or may not be reporting accurately.

To be scientifically grounded, the vocabulary must reflect current theories related to information processing and trauma, hypnosis, cognition, and memory. To be client centered, it must be focused on the client's perceptions of his or her experiences. This is a radically different perspective from one that assumes there is an objective reality that a client may or may not be presenting accurately. The truth or falsity of a disclosure is not a central concern.

This chapter will begin psychotherapy's contribution to the discourse related to memories of childhood sexual abuse. The terms defined here will be used throughout the remainder of the book.

CHILD SEXUAL ABUSE

It must be accepted that there is no universal definition of sexual abuse. This is easy to say, harder to believe—and the implications are profound. To say this another way, there is almost no human sexual behavior that is *inherently* abusive. Any behavior could be perceived as sexually abusive, and nearly any behavior could be perceived as acceptable. If this is difficult to swallow, consider that a recent review found that only eleven states have statutes that employ clear policy-guiding definitions of any type of child abuse (Howing and Wodarski, 1992). So even in one country in one specific time frame, it is impossible to achieve consensus about what constitutes sexual abuse.

There have been published calls to specify definitions of *child* abuse, but even these often ignore the need to define *sexual* abuse (e.g., Hutchison, 1993). In other words, the notion that a child can be sexually abused is such a deeply ingrained part of this culture that most people assume they know what it is. And everyone has a different definition. This does not allow a rational discussion of the topic, since any discussion has to begin with agreed-upon premises. Systematic inquiry must begin with a fundamental premise that is acceptable to scholars, clinicians, and consumers.

For the purposes of this book, *child sexual abuse will be viewed as any physical contact between a minor and any other person that the minor perceives (or comes to perceive at any point in his or her life) to be of a sexual nature and to have resulted in undesirable consequences.*

Usually child sexual abuse is defined in terms of reported behaviors. Professionals ask about what happened, when, where, and how. These kinds of details lead clinicians to an investigatory mind-set. Therapists then wonder if this "really" happened, and how it could have if, for example, the client's mother claims her uncle was out of the country when she was five, etc., etc. As has already been suggested, this type of wondering can jeopardize a therapeutic relationship.

When child sexual abuse is considered in situations in which the identified perpetrator is also a minor, the term has been defined as sexual behavior involving coercion. Ultimately, this also leads to an investigatory mind-set. Again, the therapeutic relationship is in peril.

Since this book deals with helping and not interrogation, or even investigation, specificity will be sacrificed in favor of inclusiveness. That is, if a client believes he or she was abused, the clinician must work with that belief. This definition of sexual abuse is broad, but allows the perception of the self-identified victim to be the identifying criterion.

This introduces a complication. What if the client himself or herself is unsure? There are clinical situations in which clients struggle with this uncertainty. To resolve this dilemma, the concept of memory must be reconsidered.

RE-COLLECTIONS

The concept of memory is usually considered under the assumption that it is accurate from an historical perspective. A person who remembers that it was cold and rainy on Monday comes to believe that it was, in fact, cold and rainy on Monday. The accuracy people count on in memory helps them to feel grounded in reality and gives them a connection to others in their social sphere. People go to work, for example, and say, "Thank goodness this Monday isn't cold and rainy like last Monday!" In this way, the view that memory is correct helps people to feel that reality is understandable and that the same reality is shared with others.

Sometimes, though, the feeling of a shared reality is not concrete. A question such as "Is it cold in here, or is it me?" is a kind of social gauge, a way of double-checking with others to determine whether one person's perceptions match another's perceptions. It can be troubling when they do not match. For example, it is one thing to hear a voice coming out of a stereo speaker, and it is quite another thing if no one else admits to hearing that voice.

The term "re-collection" is used here to capture a relative, storytelling function of memory. Snippets of experience are collected, pieced together, and used to relate to self and to others.

It has been demonstrated previously that memories are functional, but they are not necessarily accurate. Two siblings may have a shared story about the time they conned their mother out of five dollars, but she may remember it as the time *she* conned *them* into painting the fence. What is more important than the accuracy of the memory is the telling of the story. When do the siblings talk about the five-dollar day? Do they bond over the experience or do they feel guilty? Who does the mother tell about the fence-painting trick, and what purpose does her story serve? Does it support her contention that her children are gullible or that she has always been a resourceful parent?

The term "re-collection" is used here as a way of capturing this relative, storytelling perspective of memory. It is an attempt to symbolize the dynamic nature of the way humans appear to formulate their own memories or self-stories: we make re-collections in our relationships with others. Snippets of experience are collected, pieced together, and used as a way of relating to self and to others. Note, however, that this does not in any way trivialize the real-life events that may have affected each person's perceptions. If the five-dollar day troubles those siblings because they feel guilty for manipulating their mother, that guilt is real, whether the mother perceived the manipulation or not.

Re-collections, then, are constructed accounts of personal experiences. If a person believes an event occurred, then, for therapeutic purposes at least, it happened.

Therapists utilizing this perspective no longer get intellectually bogged down wondering whether an event really happened. Once past that barrier, clinicians and clients are free to move on in the therapeutic process.

In terms of clinical assessment, the question after "What happened?" is "Why is the client telling this story in this particular setting in this particular way?" To deliberate from this perspective, it is necessary to consider the concept of a "life narrative."

LIFE NARRATIVE

In his theory on human identity, which is based on developmental psychology and thirteen years of research on autobiographical stories, McAdams (1993) suggests that stories are the form by which we synthesize our experiences: "We each seek to provide our scattered and often confusing experiences with a sense of coherence by arranging the episodes of our lives into stories" (p. 11).

The life narrative serves a number of purposes: it is a "history of the self" (McAdams, 1993, p. 102); it is an explanation of how the past became the present; it is the personal data that serves to support the self-image. Life narratives are dynamic and ongoing and may take on the form of myth or popular drama.

Based on the work of McAdams (1993) and Hankiss (1981), life narratives are considered here to take four possible forms:

1. *Comedy*, in which a bad past gives birth to a good present
2. *Romance*, in which a good past gives birth to a good present
3. *Tragedy*, in which a bad past gives birth to a bad present
4. *Irony*, in which a good past gives birth to a bad present

Thus, the person who strives to create a life narrative that includes childhood sexual abuse most often must choose between the construction of a comedy or a tragedy. A comedy will include an ending in which the storyteller is perceived to be in control of personal destiny, responsible for his or her own actions. A bad past that leads to a good present supports a survivor's self-image. On the other hand, a tragedy finds the storyteller powerless—the person had no power over a bad past and therefore has no power over the bad present. Hence, the person is not responsible for his or her actions and is generally helpless—someone who maintains a self-image of "victim."

In other words, *the life narrative is the story an individual tells both self and others. It is a story that helps to define that individual's identity.* If the individual is comfortable with the life narrative, he or she is comfortable with the definition of self it depicts. For comfort to be maintained, the story will necessarily be altered depending upon a shifting social context. Some aspects of identity, for example, are highlighted when speaking with friends, others are highlighted in work-related interactions, and still others are highlighted with family members. Stories about experiences serve to clarify and emphasize an individual's identity.

The life narrative is constructed not just in the face of this everchanging world but in conjunction with it. Thus, each person's life narrative is "subjugated to serve the dominant discourse, which comes to define a culture and maintain the status quo" (Parry and Doan, 1994, p. 17). This viewpoint highlights the importance of the social factors that affect the definition of a life experience as traumatic, benign, or life enhancing. It also highlights the potential importance of assisting vulnerable populations to find a voice and become authors of their own stories, which will ultimately affect the discourse of the entire culture.

Both individual and social factors affect the definition of a life experience as traumatic, benign, or life enhancing.

Life narratives give life intelligibility and create a meaningful continuum over the life span. The quality of intentionality "makes it possible for people to plot the course of their lives according to their own choices" (Parry and Doan, 1994, p. 3). Thus, telling one's own story with a conscious eye toward one's own intentions places the power of potential change firmly in the storyteller's hands.

It is important to note here that although narrative, myth, and stories are not the only method individuals and cultures have for making meaning, they are significant vehicles for this endeavor (Hall, 1981). This presents particular challenges for persons who identify themselves as sexual abuse survivors. It has been suggested that survivors of abuse face so many obstacles to verbalizations about feelings that contact with emotions is lost and the ability to create narratives about the emotions is lost as well. For these persons, simply finding a voice to create and express their narratives to themselves and others becomes a major goal of therapy. Nonverbal therapeutic modalities such as art and movement have been suggested as a way of creating a "bridge between the unspoken and spoken, between the unknown and the known" (Simonds, 1994, p. 1).

Again, therapists are faced with the importance of the first-time telling of the tale. For the abuse survivor, the life narrative has many missing pages—stories too painful to think about, let alone tell. In these situations, the therapist plays an important role in facilitating the first-time telling in a safe and productive way.

"SELF"

It is significant that for the postmodern, narrative perspective, self exists in a reciprocal relationship with both environment and life story. *Self, in other words, is one's own definition of identity— the leading character in an ever-unfolding life story.* Since the life story is created by the individual in concert with the social milieu, it is both acceptable and adaptable that both the story and the self would change in different contexts. This is particularly relevant for the population of adults who come to view themselves as survivors of childhood sexual abuse, since the personal experience of multiple selves (or multiple personalities) has traditionally been considered to be pathological and maladaptive rather than acceptable and adaptive. Take note that gender-neutral language is used here, as elsewhere throughout this book. This choice is made particularly since the problem of new re-collections of decades-old incidents of sexual abuse is probably not limited to the experience of women (Gasker, 1993).

The notion of the development of multiple selves for adaptive behavior in multiple worlds is attractive. Still, there is a very human need to perceive one's self as consistent. The individual's own perception of himself or herself must be comfortable to be functional. If self-perception is so multiple as to be fragmented, so situation dependent as to be inconsistent, it can deteriorate into psychopathology.

Characteristics of the healthy self:

1. *The self is the creation of the author of the life story.*
2. *The self is consistent yet adaptable to changing social conditions and additional life experiences.*
3. *The self is validated, or acknowledged, by significant others.*

Here, narrative theory provides a helpful perspective. This perspective considers the life narrative to be a reciprocal creator of self. Although subject to revision in the presence of changing individual and social conditions, it nevertheless provides a coherent sense of self.

This sense of self—born of a life narrative that is at once changeable, a product of one's own agency, and a consistent and accurate portrayal of self—may be fostered by a therapist. To foster this sense of self, the therapist must be willing to validate a client relating stories through his or her own perspective without wondering about the historical accuracy of those stories.

Repression and dissociation have come to be associated with the true-versus-false debate concerning adult recollections of childhood sexual abuse.

DIS-INTEGRATED RE-COLLECTION

A dis-integrated re-collection is a life experience that is disconnected from the life story. This term has been chosen to replace such concepts as "repression" and "dissociation."

There are many potential problems with the use of the terms repression and dissociation. As has been demonstrated, these more traditional terms are often used interchangeably and have been defined differently by different theorists. In addition, repression and dissociation have come to be associated closely with the true-versus-false debate concerning adult re-collections of childhood sexual abuse. While one school of thought considers the concept of dissociation to be potentially harmful and the identification of various dissociated selves "about as useful as rearranging deck chairs on the Titanic" (Ganaway, 1993), another suggests that dissociative splits within the treatment process ought to be allowed for, "even encouraged" (Davies and Frawley, 1994, p. 201). The field of psychiatry continues to be divided on whether dissociative disorders are "culturally specific" to the United States or whether increases in reporting indicate greater awareness of the disorders among mental health professionals (American Psychiatric Association, 1994, p. 484).

Among the recent literature on dissociation is a collection of works (Lynn and Rhue, 1994) that attempts to bridge a number of theories regarding multiple personality disorder and the development of historically inaccurate memories. This work has been successful to the extent that it has been favorably reviewed by both Theodore Sarbin, a founder of narrative psychology, and Campbell Perry, a recognized expert in hypnosis. Contributors include Elizabeth Loftus and David Spiegel. Some difficulties with the use of the term dissociation are highlighted by the text. These difficulties include the concept's potential influence on the social and biological aspects of dissociation. For example, it is suggested that trauma causes chemical changes which result in a unique type of memory, the treatment of which ought to be desensitization, as well as exploration of the idea that multiple personality disorder may be socially constructed, created by dreams and the transference-countertransference phenomenon, or even encouraged by the very tests used to determine its existence (Lynn and Rhue, 1994).

A new paradigm has been suggested to replace the traditional use of dissociation as a way of understanding the impact of trauma.

Ultimately, a new paradigm—"traumatergic"—has been suggested, in which the impact of trauma on personality development is viewed less as a dissociation, or splitting up of parts of the self, and more as a "complex phenomenon involving the development of alternative versions of the self to adapt to unrelenting and unremediated trauma . . ." (Lynn and Rhue, 1994, p. 445).

The self is known through narrative.

Thus, alternative versions of the self—rather than the traumatic history—may become the focus of inquiry. It has been suggested (Schafer, 1992) that the self is known through narrative and that this process inherently includes more than one single self-entity; for example, "I told myself to get going" is to "tell a self story with two characters" (p. 27).

Qualities of Dis-Integrated Re-Collections:

- *Do not fit comfortably into the life story*
- *May be experienced as painful memories*
- *May be experienced as alternative versions of the self, e.g., "multiple personalities"*
- *May be unconscious most of the time*
- *May present cognitive dissonance, or discomfort, when conscious*
- *May never have been disclosed to another person*
- *May have been disclosed and invalidated, i.e., viewed as misunderstandings, exaggerations, or outright lies*
- *May intrude into consciousness suddenly and unexpectedly in the form of flashbacks or nightmares*

Dis-integrated re-collection will be used here to refer to any re-collection of a perceived experience that has not been integrated into the life story. That is, these are stories about life events or aspects of self-entities that do not fit comfortably into the overall life story. They may be experienced as isolated "memories." They may be developed to a greater or lesser extent as "alternative" versions of the self or may remain for the most part unconscious.

Dis-integrated re-collections are likely to present some discomfort or cognitive dissonance when they are conscious, since they have not been easily incorporated into the life story. These re-collections may not have been shared with a trusted other. On the other hand, they may have been disclosed in a social interaction, only to be invalidated by a perceived authority figure. For the period during which the re-collection has not been integrated into the life story, the holder of the re-collection may or may not be aware of it. It may be unconscious for much or all of the time, perhaps intruding into consciousness suddenly and unexpectedly, as one study participant put it, "just popping up whenever."

EPIPHANY EXPERIENCE

An epiphany is an eye-opening event. Traditionally, this term refers to the Magi recognizing the divinity of the Christ child. Thus, an epiphany is a significant event, a turning point in a life. For Denzin (1989), an epiphany is a problematic interactional situation in which an individual confronts and experiences some kind of crisis. The epiphany experience may leave positive or negative marks on a person's life.

Denzin (1989) does not stress, however, the individual's power in selecting life experiences to identify as epiphanies, or turning points. According to McAdams (1993), an individual does have that power. Here, the epiphany experience will be similar to McAdams's "nuclear episode" (pp. 293ff). For the purposes of this book, *the epiphany experience is a re-collection that comes to take on prominence in the life narrative.* These experiences may be high points, low points, or turning points in the course of life.

Epiphanies are experiences chosen to be symbolic events in the life story.

It is important to note that no experiences are inherently high points or low points. They are not necessarily even perceived as significant when they occur. In the life story, however, they come to be symbolic—perhaps of continuity in the self-image, perhaps of change in the self-image.

Denzin's definition of epiphany does, on the other hand, make a significant point: the epiphany is dynamic. These life turning points change over time and in different situations: "Epiphanies are group, interactional phenomena. These stories are given multiple meanings, by the person [narrator] and others. Their meanings change over time" (Denzin, 1989, p. 40). To consider the dynamic nature of the epiphany and its place in the life narrative, the process of integration is delineated next.

INTEGRATION

Integration is the process of fitting an experience into the life narrative. This involves framing the experience in terms that are congruent with the self-image being supported by the life story.

The therapist acts as editor and helps the client write a functional life story.

A congruent life story that includes the traumatic event is the goal of the helping process. The therapist acts as editor and helps the client write a functional, integrated story of his or her self. The functional story may include traumatic events, but these events are framed as negative past experiences that have helped shape the characteristics of the strong, healthy self in the present.

DISCLOSURE ISSUES

Chapter 3

From Disclosure to Integration: Processing Re-Collections of Sexual Abuse

Though we may act out parts of our personal myth in daily life, the story is inside of us. It is made and remade in the secrecy of our own minds, both conscious and unconscious, and for our own psychological discovery and enjoyment. In moments of great intimacy, we may share important episodes with another person. . . . We do not discover ourselves in myth; we make ourselves through myth. Truth is constructed in the midst of our loving and hating; our tasting, smelling, and feeling; our daily appointments and weekend lovemaking; in the conversations we have with those to whom we are closest; and with the stranger we meet on the bus. Stories from antiquity provide some raw materials for personal mythmaking, but not necessarily more than the television sitcoms we watch in prime time. Our sources are wildly varied, and our possibilities, vast . . .

(McAdams, 1993, pp. 12, 13)

Once an experience has been defined as a traumatic incident of childhood sexual abuse, it is potentially harmful to the quality of life. To answer the question, "What might therapists do to use clients' traumatic re-collections to improve the quality of their lives?" a consideration of life narrative construction is necessary.

This chapter includes a provisional model of the process of integrating a traumatic event into the life story. (See Figure 3.1.) It is based on empirical study as well as a logical extension of the available literature. The model demonstrates the entire integration process and highlights the importance of various aspects of the initial disclosure.

FIGURE 3.1. Reaching Resolution: The Process of Integrating Trauma into the Life Narrative

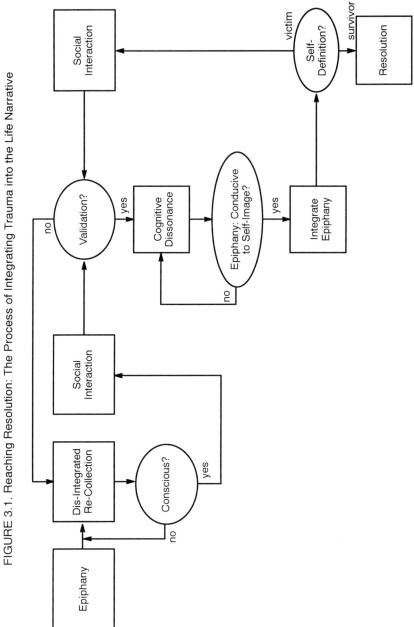

> *To answer the question, "What might therapists do to help clients use their re-collections of trauma to improve the quality of their lives?" a consideration of life narrative construction is necessary.*

A THEORY OF RE-COLLECTION

The Integration Process

The integration of an epiphany experience into the life narrative appears to occur in a process. This process is developmental; that is, one stage builds upon another.

> *At some point, the re-collection bearer looks at his or her life and realizes a sexually abusive event has taken place.*

Epiphany Experience

The process of integrating an event into the life story begins with an epiphany experience. This experience can be any social event, but for the present purpose it is assumed to be one that has come to be defined by the holder of the experience as an instance of childhood sexual abuse. At some point, the re-collection bearer looks at his or her life and realizes that a sexually abusive event has occurred. This can happen while the event is occurring or it can happen decades later. It might happen as a result of a flashback, a disturbing experience, or a conscious effort toward introspection, but the ultimate result is the new belief, "I may have experienced sexual abuse!"

Dis-Integrated Re-Collection

Once an experience is perceived as being one of sexual abuse, it takes on the characteristics of dis-integration. That is, it is not an insignificant life event that may carelessly be forgotten. Instead, it pushes its way into the bearer's consciousness with varying frequency, demanding validation.

> *The re-collection of the abusive event pushes its way into the bearer's consciousness, demanding validation.*

The urgency of the demand for validation varies depending upon a myriad of personal and interpersonal factors. For example, discomfort seems to increase based on the length of time the secret is kept as well as in the presence of ongoing invalidation. With such discomfort, the re-collection bearer is caught in a mire of anxiety: the dis-integrated re-collection demands validation, but the bearer fears taking the risk of potential invalidation by attempting to share it with someone who may not be "safe," or trustworthy.

> *The re-collection may literally force its way into the bearer's consciousness through flashbacks or nightmares.*

At this stage, the re-collection may literally force its way into the bearer's consciousness through sudden intrusions in the form of flashbacks or troubling dreams. Persons may experience these sudden flashes of awareness privately or in the therapeutic setting. In either case, the re-collection bearer will seek to share the experience to gain the sought-after validation.

> *The validation of an experience requires a relationship with a trusted other.*

Interaction with a Trusted Other

The validation of an experience requires a relationship with a trusted other. When the validation of an abuse story is being sought, the re-collection bearer takes his or her experience to one or more others. Through interaction with those persons, the reality of the experience is defined. Since the social context has affected a definition of trauma, the assumption is that a potentially harmful event has taken place. Thus, a logical extension of the data recorded here suggests that a client's search for validation is a way of beginning to determine whether his or her life is a tragedy, in which a bad past leads to a bad present, or a comedy, in which a bad past leads to a good present.

The search for validation is the beginning of the choice between a life story that is a comedy and one that is a tragedy.

The Significance of Validation

The validation process is significant for a number of reasons, based on this study and others regarding persons who perceive themselves as survivors of sexual abuse. First, they may have few or no trusted others in their lives, resulting in a long-held secret. Holding the secret, the unvalidated portion of the life story, as a dis-integrated experience is accomplished at the expense of varying degrees of psychic energy. The secret demands validation; the dis-integrated portion of the life story demands integration. This dis-integrated experience may manifest itself in some form of dissociative symptoms.

Invalidation may be experienced as secondary trauma.

Second, the validation process is significant because it appears that women and men who have traumatic re-collections may have significant others in their lives who actively *in*validate their traumatic experiences. This invalidation may be accomplished by outright denial or by more subtle forms of manipulation that serve to insist that the experience was not traumatic or was somehow caused by the victim. This invalidation may be experienced as a secondary trauma by the victim.

Finally, the validation process is significant in that it is affected by the degree of trust, the closeness of the relationship, and the level of authority the potentially validating person holds in the life of the re-collection bearer. The significance of the validation is great due to the likelihood that the victim has few trusted persons in his or her life with whom to share troubling experiences.

The initial disclosure of a re-collection of abuse is the most delicate moment in the helping process.

For a re-collection bearer even to seek validation, there must be a feeling of trust and closeness. Because validation is so central to the healing process, the potential listener has a great deal of power over the re-collection bearer.

When the potential listener is a therapist, this issue of power and authority is compounded. The therapist has the power and the professional sanction to label the re-collection bearer as a person who suffers from mental illness. This authority makes the risk even greater for the client who is seeking validation. Yet, many take the risk because the need for validation is so emotionally pressing.

This is the most delicate moment in the helping relationship with sexual abuse survivors: the leap of faith has been taken; the story has been told—will it be validated?

The Face of Validation

Again, validation as described by Sands (1996) includes accepting the client's role as narrator and consequently accepting his or her perspective as valid, respecting the choice not to divulge certain details and accepting the identity the narrative depicts for the narrator. This atmosphere of acceptance seems to be the "safe" place survivors stress as so important to recovery from abuse. If a validating person is not found, the experience continues to be pushed into consciousness, particularly in periods of stress.

The Clinical Faces of Validation:

- *The client is viewed as narrator, author, and owner of the life story being told*
- *The client's perception is accepted as valid*
- *The client chooses freely which details to include, and which to omit*
- *The client defines the identity of self in the life story being told*

Ongoing Invalidation

It appears that a situation characterized by either no validation at all or active invalidation is extremely harmful to the formulation of a positive self-image. For example, the three members of the therapy group studied seemed to have three distinctly different types of resolutions to their situations. Beth told a long-held secret story within the group. Without anyone specifically telling her they believed the story, her feelings about it were validated. Following the group process, she felt that her attendance was very beneficial and that the most important aspect for her was the sharing of the secret in a safe environment. In the postgroup interview she stated that keeping the secret had been "tearing [her] apart."

On the other hand, Catherine shared a secret for the first time within the group, but her integration of the story into her life narrative did not appear to be possible. She became increasingly anxious during the duration of the group and for one month following its termination. Shortly thereafter, she was admitted to an inpatient psychiatric facility for evaluation due to her periods of withdrawal and bouts of unexplainable screaming. One significant difference between Beth's situation and Catherine's is that Catherine was experiencing ongoing invalidation. She had stated during the group that her sister remained friends with the son of the perpetrator and that this friendship made her very uncomfortable. In the follow-up interview, she brought up the situation with her sister and this friendship again and expressed her anger at the ongoing invalidation:

Catherine: But I haven't made this . . . up [the abuse story]. Because—Elaine [Catherine's sister] doesn't know—remember when I was with her. But I do. That's the time when . . . [unintelligible] . . . really, really late coming back. And the things started . . .

Interviewer: Do you think—is this the kind of thing you can get over? Can you get better?

Catherine: I don't think so.

Interviewer: You just have to deal with it?

Catherine: Yeah.

Finally, Charlene was not able to come to any resolution concerning her abuse story at all, perhaps because she was not able to share it with the group. When she was interviewed about her reasons for dropping out of the group, she stated that she did not feel that she could discuss her story in any group setting, but also indicated that she would like to do so. While she had little insight about the reasons for her inability to tell her story, further into the interview she described a situation in which family members supplied almost immediate and continuous invalidation of her abuse:

> **Charlene:**   [in the context of discussing the experience of having her brother-in-law's child and having that child adopted by another sister] . . . my mother said [to me], "We've had one 'mistake' [in the family]; let's not have any more . . . "

When asked about her father's reaction to the birth of her child, Charlene stated that her father was upset only a short time. "Then he was so excited to have a grandson—he wanted a grandson."

She also pointed out, without prompting, the effects the ongoing invalidation had on her current functioning. She had recently experienced acute discomfort at a family gathering. Current holidays, thirteen years after the abuse, are still difficult because she has to be in the presence of her abuser:

> Holidays . . . I hafta go to this person's house . . . Kinda like a relative—and—it's very—I feel very uncomfortable . . . I had a dress on yesterday and my dress was not short or anything but I felt uncomfortable. So I had—I was sitting like—yeah— So I had—I was sitting like—yeah—So I was like—like I had something over my lap because I felt, you know, like I had a sweater or something covering my legs because I felt very— very uncomfortable.

In addition, Charlene's health concerns may have been another manifestation of her inability to have her re-collections validated. When she viewed the tape of the session in which she struggled unsuccessfully to tell her story, Charlene noted that when the topic of sexual abuse was brought up she began to eat and drink. When questioned about whether overeating may have been tied to the potential discussion of abuse, she said she believed it had. In a surprised tone, she exclaimed, "I guess it [eating] makes me shut up!"

Validation, Not Inflammation

It should be reiterated here that validation does not necessarily involve a process of acknowledging the truth or historical accuracy of an account of an event. In this research, it was observed that in order to validate a re-collection, it does not appear to be necessary to agree that the event occurred. In addition, it is not necessary to join in an evaluation of the devastating nature of the experience. Instead, it is necessary to take the report seriously, hold it in confidence if requested, and acknowledge the emotion that has come to surround the event.

While studies have suggested that the most severe forms of abuse and abusive situations that last longest have the most deleterious consequences (Finkelhor et al., 1990; Peters, 1988), the consequences of ongoing invalidation do not seem to have been empirically evaluated. This is a significant issue in work with this population, especially since the assumption that the therapist must take abuse re-collections to be historical fact is at the foundation of the recovered memories debate. Again, it appears that the feelings expressed by the client need to be validated by the therapist, while discussions of the historical accuracy of the abuse reports is frequently tangential to the therapeutic work.

Validating an Abuse Re-Collection

Don't:

- *Affirm belief in the historical accuracy of the event reported*
- *Pronounce the damaging effects likely to result from the experience*

Do:

- *Take the report seriously*
- *Hold the report in confidence*

- *Acknowledge emotions associated with the re-collection*
- *Provide a present-oriented focus on the current life story*

Dissonance

Once validation occurs, relief from stress is not imminent. In fact, study participants reported a period of acute discomfort just following validation of an abuse disclosure. A logical extension of this data suggests that this discomfort is likely to be caused by the sense of cognitive dissonance that results from having the abuse experience validated as real.

Once a re-collection is validated, dissonance occurs, a feeling of acute emotional discomfort that survivors say represents the need to put back together the pieces of their lives.

The experience now requires a place in the life story. Dissonance is the feeling of discomfort abuse survivors describe as the need to put together the pieces of their lives. Integrating an experience into the life narrative requires a self-image check. The experience must either be framed in a way that supports the current self-image, or the self-image must be altered to fit the emerging life story. Note that the emerging self-image and the emerging life narrative are engaged in an interactive relationship: each affects the other in an ongoing reciprocal relationship rather than one being caused by the other.

Beth struggled during the first few weeks of group with rage and what she perceived as misdirected and uncontrollable anger. Later on, however, she expressed an emerging sense of control. During one interview prior to group, she expressed her re-collection sharing as a conscious choice made toward personal growth and discussed an emerging change in time orientation. In addition, she stated that she felt better able to control her experiences of spontaneous re-collection of abuse events:

> **Interviewer:** What are your impressions of group?
> **Beth:**   Umm. (7 seconds) It's helping me out a lot. About my past. Umm. (7 seconds) That I'm just

thinking about my future now. 'Stead of my past all the time—some of the times.

Factors Influencing Comedy and Tragedy

The findings reported here point tentatively toward possible factors that may influence whether the life story which includes a re-collection of sexual abuse develops into a comedy or tragedy. Further study is needed to better understand this process and ultimately design effective intervention techniques.

In this society, an experience that is perceived as one of childhood sexual abuse is likely to become an epiphany, or turning point, in the life story. Whether this epiphany turns the life narrative into a comedy or a tragedy seems to depend on the interaction of a number of individual and social factors.

Therapeutic Goals for Life Narratives That Include Traumatic Re-Collections:

1. The story must be credible as it is told to others.
2. The narrator must be able to adjust the story slightly to fit the context of the telling.
3. The story must be that of a survivor, not a victim.
4. The story should be told by a person who feels in control of the present environment and of the creation of the story itself.

When the life narrative includes an epiphany story of childhood sexual abuse, the goal of therapy is to have this story told in a way that accomplishes several individual and social goals. First, the story must be credible as it is told in various contexts, and the narrator must be able to adjust the telling to make it both acceptable and credible in the context; second, the story must be a comedy. In the childhood sexual abuse story that is a comedy, the narrator plays the role of survivor, not victim.

The status of survivor seems to entail a few conditions. First, it is a dynamic role. Survivors say they believe survivors of sexual abuse do not ever "get over it"; instead they learn to cope with it. Second, the role of survivor is focused on a sense of mastery in the present environment. Therapeutic discussion about emotional safety, which clients often insist includes physical safety, is indicative of their ongoing concern with this issue.

Integration: The Therapeutic Goal

A life story in which the abuse experiences are integrated in a manner that supports a positive self-image and one in which control over one's life is a theme should be the goal of treatment. It is important to note that a sense of mastery over one's own life may begin with the telling of the life story itself, if it is done with the recognition that the teller is the author.

The first step, then, in recognizing the power of authorship in one's own life story is the experience of telling it in a safe environment. The next step is recognizing that one might be a competent author. Evidence of this recognition may be the movement of a traumatic story to the context of current events. When the life story is focused in the present, it necessarily takes on a dynamic aspect in which the teller alters it to suit the environment and the audience.

Managing the all-important initial disclosure in a validating, therapeutic fashion is the beginning of the helping process . . .

Therapeutic Direction

In conclusion, the integrating process begins with an epiphany experience that may or may not occur in the therapeutic setting. Following that experience is the client's all-important search for validation. This stage in the process is quite likely to lead to the therapist's office. Managing that initial disclosure in a validating, therapeutic fashion is the beginning of the helping process with survivors of sexual trauma and is the focus of the following chapters.

Chapter 4

First-Time Stories:
The Structure of Therapy

The process of integration described in the previous chapter high-lights the importance of the initial disclosure, the first-time telling of an abuse story. This is the interactional moment of truth: the client is risking all by sharing this story. As we have seen, a therapist's response that a client perceives as invalidating might cause untold damage as well as forfeiting the therapeutic relationship. On the other hand, a premature response might plagiarize the story, making it the therapist's, not the client's.

An invalidating response to a first-time disclosure of an abuse re-collection may forfeit the therapeutic relationship.

Incidents in which first-time disclosures of childhood sexual abuse were shared in the therapeutic milieu are highlighted in this chapter. The disclosures occurred in a small therapy group. Recurrent themes that emerged from the analysis of field notes, interviews, and video-tapes are identified and described. The group consisted of a master's-level therapist and three female members. For details regarding the group's composition, setting, and context, see the Appendix.

. . . while a premature response might plagiarize the story, making it the therapist's, not the client's.

A group setting was chosen as a vehicle to analyze abuse disclo-sures due to the wealth of interactions available in a group. With only three members and a facilitator, this particular group is also simple to understand in terms of individuals and their contributions. In the passages of this chapter, the therapist is called Sandra, while group members have been assigned the pseudonyms Catherine, Beth, and Charlene.

FIRST-TIME DISCLOSURE IN THE GROUP SETTING

In this group for survivors of sexual trauma, the members discussed specific stories of abuse almost immediately, even though the facilitator did not encourage or even expect this to happen. "I was blown away," she said later. The following sections examine closely the way in which this disclosure occurred and the interactional strategies that allowed it to happen.

Members discussed specific stories of abuse almost immediately, even though the facilitator did not encourage it.

Group Structure

Here the group structure is reported by topic and significant events. The information has been gleaned from field notes and videotapes, and triangulated with session follow-up notes provided by the facilitator to group participants through the mail each week to improve continuity. Since each of these group members complained of memory difficulties, the facilitator also included a reiteration of the week's homework assignments in the weekly follow-up notes.

Structure of Sessions

Table 4.1 illustrates the structure that was generally common to all group sessions. The table also identifies and highlights the context of incidents of participants' re-collections of childhood sexual abuse. The length of each major part of the group meetings is noted as a range, from the shortest length of that particular section to the longest that section lasted throughout the group series.

TABLE 4.1. Structure of Sessions

The Period of Contact (duration 85-122 minutes)		
Social Period	**Work Phase** **Social Work Group Treatment**	**Closing Routine**
4-38 min.	43-56 min. (break 3-13) 19-35 min.	2-10 min.

Principal Parts

Review / Processing / Current Concerns Break / Psychoeducation / Assignment

Primary Discourse Topics

family, pets, current events (esp. violence), food, joking	contracting, review, experiential exercise, safety, trust, coping with emotions, relationships, abuse story, and current ramifications

Constituent Conversation Routines

1. EXPLAIN (W) 2. attending (c) 1. questioning (W) 2. answering (c) 3. REFLECTING, REFRAMING, NOTING, TEACH-ING, REINFORCING, NORMALIZING, ASSIGNING HOMEWORK, REACHING FOR FEELINGS, IDENTI-FYING FEELINGS (W) 4. written activity, SELF-DISCLOSURE, facilitating transitions (W), (c)

(c) = client
(W) = worker
UPPERCASE = foregrounded activity
* = re-collections of abuse stories

Each week, the entire period of contact lasted approximately two hours. After the first session, the group began with a social period, which the facilitator designed to accommodate the public transportation schedule as well as to provide a relaxed atmosphere. The formal work period of the group lasted between sixty-two and ninety-one minutes, with a short break midgroup.

Principal Parts

The principal parts of each group followed a regular pattern. Each week's formal group work began with a review of the prior week's topics of concern. This was followed by the facilitator opening up the group to current day-to-day concerns—the "How was your week?" section. After discussing here-and-now coping exercises for current concerns, a short break followed. This was a time to use the bathroom or refill a coffee cup. The second half of group consisted of a period of psychoeducation on a topic introduced by the facilitator. This period also included the experiential drawing exercises and the assignment of homework tasks.

Discourse Topics

During the pregroup social time, a handful of topics were introduced throughout the group experience informally by the members and facilitator. These included family issues, usually reports of visits to relatives or news about immediate family members; current events, especially those related to violent crimes occurring in the city in which the group met; group snacks and other logistics; and some good-natured joking between the members and the facilitator. The researcher participated in these informal discussion periods, but only peripherally. This was a conscious decision; it would have been awkward not to speak at all, but undesirable to heavily influence the conversation. Minimal involvement in the informal socialization periods was accomplished by making adjustments to video and audio equipment.

One session included an informal interview between the members and the researcher during the pregroup period. The researcher took the opportunity to individually interview the group members on tape on an occasion when the group facilitator was late in arriving.

The formal group period included contracting and review of previous topics. Overall, these topics included trust, safety, significant relationships, emotional coping, and the current ramifications of sexual abuse histories.

Each specific discussion of re-collections of childhood sexual abuse occurred in the period following break. There were eleven discussions in which specific stories were told, eight in the first session and three in the third session. Other conversations about sexual abuse histories occurred only in the context of what current life situations might be influenced by the histories and were not expressed as accounts of what had happened. For example, it was considered to be a story in the context of the present—not an account of what had happened per se—when Catherine tied her abuse history to a period of promiscuity by saying, "He set me a bad example."

Constituent Conversation Routines

The conversational routines that occurred during the formal work of the group were quite stable. Each group began with a contracting period in which the facilitator verbally laid out a rough plan for the group and offered the members an opportunity to influence the plan. Members attended closely to her plan but did not offer suggestions for changes. Other sections of group began with the facilitator initiating discussion by asking an open-ended question; in this way, she gave members an opportunity to determine the focus of discussion. One or more group members would answer, usually directing their responses to the facilitator. The discussion would then continue with the facilitator using a number of possible social work interventions: summing up, identifying feelings, clarifying comments, and noting on an easel, teaching, normalizing, reflecting, and reframing. Other conversational routines included the assignment of tasks and the facilitation of transitions from one routine to another.

The first-time disclosures appeared suddenly in conversation, seemingly out of context.

An Exception

An exception to these conversational routines was the specific, first-time disclosures of sexual abuse histories, which did not occur in response to a question from the facilitator. The first-time disclosures appeared suddenly in conversation, seemingly out of context. For example, Beth's initial attempt to discuss the part of her abuse history that included intercourse with a younger brother follows. She is describing her drawing during the group's first experiential activity, but she actually describes what she did *not* draw rather than what she did draw:

Sandra: How about you, Beth? Tell us a little bit about your—your [drawing of a] storage box.

Beth: Umm, I didn't put my brother in here though.

Sandra: I'm sorry?

Beth: My brother. My youngest brother. Larry. Umm, I never told my mom or my dad—he wanted to have sex with me and I was like late in my teenagers—age—and I'm afraid if he was gonna hit me—er—(4 seconds) do something—and—I was afraid of him. I just failed to put that down on the paper also.

Structure of Groups by Discussion Topics

In addition to noting the structure of the therapy and where disclosures occurred within that structure, these groups were analyzed by discussion topic. Table 4.2 provides a composite of the entire group series with a focus on the topics discussed. The six sessions are divided into sections: the pregroup social time; the two major work phases of each group, which surrounded a brief break period; and the short postgroup exiting time.

Introductory Session

With the exception of the re-collections of abuse that members occasionally interjected into sessions, most group work periods covered topics as planned by the facilitator. Group rules were articulated during this first session by members, with the facilitator providing focus and direction. Significantly, group members initiated the issue of confidentiality, which was elaborated upon at length by the facilitator. The facilitator proceeded to explain group purpose, and she requested that members share their goals for attending. Members discussed ways of coping with disturbing re-collections as they came up unexpectedly during the week.

TABLE 4.2. Group Discussion Topics

Session	Pregroup Social Time	Work Phase I	Break	Work Phase II	Postgroup
1	Consent forms (B,C); Position taping equip. 25 min.	Intro.; Expect.; Rules; Feelings drawing activity 47 min.	Family, location Snack Restroom 7 min.	First-time abuse stories; Coping; Trust 26 min.	Trust; Member check 3 min.
2	Consent form (C) Joking, movies, clothes, family; Payment; B. presents snack; Handouts 25 min.	Journal: intro., self-esteem; Trust; Coping; Safety 52 min.	Snack Writing task 10 min.	Safety: physical and emotion; Close group to new members; Goal setting; Drawing task 30 min.	Crafts; Member check (B) 14 min.
3	Joking, location; B. has pressing issue; Handouts 14 min.	Changes; Trust; Memory problem; Coping; Relax. exercise 52 min.	Family, pets; Snack; Restroom 15 min.	Feelings; Results of Abuse; Task Assign.: Feelings 35 min.	Family; Member check (W) 10 min.
4	Informal inter. (W): concern with C's staff; Family, weather; Location 15 min.	Anger; Review of task assign.: Trust 48 min.	Work, family, shopping; Snack; Restroom 10 min.	Safety; Collage; Task 43 min.	Member check: (W) 15 min.
5	Group eval. (B,C) 25 min. Family, pets, friends, vacation 37 min.	Results of abuse: memory, self-esteem, std's, substance abuse 44 min.	Family; Snack; Restroom 6 min.	Review and cont. collage: trust, results of abuse, strength 32 min.	Member check: (W) 12 min.
6	Family, location 3 min.	Current concern: men, med. test Handout; Problem Solving; Review; Eval. 52 min.	Planning c. 10 min	Goodbyes at diner c. 30 min	Parting

---
Group members initiated the topic of confidentiality.

An experiential drawing exercise was completed in group, leading to the week's most significant event: members drew pictures related to abuse scenarios and freely told stories about childhood sexual abuse. Sandra initiated the exercise in the following way:

> How would you feel about doing some drawing?—What I'm hoping to do is give you a different way to express what's inside. Sometimes people think you need to talk about it— sometimes you can't put it into words. So I brought this huge paper—I have tons of markers—and I'd like you guys to think about something that's inside that might be in a box and—you don't have to tell me what's inside the box—but draw a picture of what it feels like. It could be about anything. It could be about work. It can be about a memory. It can be about being here—about what it feels like to be here. See what you come up with.

After a period of twenty minutes of intense concentration by the group members, Sandra suggested the group take a short break and discuss their drawings afterward. A few minutes later, Catherine began discussing her anxieties about her drawing experience even though Sandra had not shifted the group from break to official group work. This was the only occasion during the entire group series in which a member disturbed the planned course of events by introducing a group topic during the prescribed social experience of break.

This was the only occasion in the entire group series when a member disrupted the planned course of events . . .

Catherine was bursting with anxiety about telling her secret. She stated that she had experienced abuse in the form of involuntary intercourse with the father of her sister's boyfriend when she was twelve years old. She repeated that she had never shared the story with anyone but her sister, who urged her not to tell. Again and again, she expressed her discomfort with breaking her promise to her sister:

> **C:** (to Sandra) We might as well start talking about this (pointing to picture) now.
>
> **S:** Okay. How about when you're—kinda done snacking we could talk about it?
>
> **C:** I just hope my sister doesn't hate me.
>
> **S:** Sounds like you're worried about that.
>
> **C:** Yeah.
>
> **S:** Do you want to talk about it now, or do you want to wait till you're done eating?
>
> **C:** Wait.
>
> **B:** (Begins brief discussion about her drawing technique.)
>
> **C:** I'm just afraid she'll hate me for the rest of my life.
>
> **S:** Hopefully, one of the things we can do in here is talk about ways to deal with the worry part of things.
>
> **C:** She told me not to say anything to anybody.
>
> **S:** Sounds like she asked you to keep a secret.
>
> **C:** Um-hum.
>
> **B:** This looks like vanilla and chocolate (continuing to attend to the doughnut she is having over break time).
>
> **S:** The icing?
>
> **B:** (Begins small talk with W, C participates in a one-minute conversation about B's extended family.)
>
> **C:** (Out of current context) But what hurts me the most, Sandra, is that my mom and dad didn't find out. They never will. So, I tell my sister—"Who breaks first, me or you?"
>
> **S:** You talking about what you put in your picture?
>
> **C:** Yeah. So my mom is gonna eventually find out.
>
> **S:** Do you want to start talking about it? It seems like it's hard for you to be relaxed—maybe if you start talking about it a little bit we can get an idea about what you're worried about, and you can tell us about your picture at the same time . . .

---

*Group members found emotional and physical safety to be synony-
mous, perhaps because they have come to feel both emotionally and
physically unsafe and therefore equate the two.*

A Safe Place

In the second group session re-collections were not discussed.
Group basics were reviewed, and Sandra initiated a discussion and
written exercise about safety. She intended to discuss emotional
safety, that is, finding and talking to trusted or safe others in an
environment of acceptance. She was surprised to learn that group
members found emotional and physical safety to be synonymous.
The facilitator's interpretation of this was that the participants have
only the intellectual abilities needed to process concrete concepts. It
may, however, be too simplistic to assume that they are too limited
intellectually to understand the ambiguous concept of emotional
safety. Another explanation is that they have come to feel vulnerable both emotionally and physically, and they consequently equate
the two. It was during this session that the three women, who were
already acquainted, decided they would like to limit the group
membership to themselves. The group facilitator agreed to honor
that decision despite the limited financial return to her relative to the
group.

The issue of safety and its ties to trust and relationship have been
important to the group clinician who runs therapy groups in an
intensive outpatient mental health clinic in the same area. In an
informal interview, she stated that many of her clients tell her that
they have revealed their abuse histories for the first time in her
groups. She believes that since group work is very limited in the
psychiatric hospital environment and short patient stays mean little
ongoing contact with other patients, groups are important to the
disclosure process. "I think they need a safe environment," she
said, "where they know they won't be attacked or blown off" (A.
Pierre, personal communication, April 13, 1995).

Likewise, it has been suggested elsewhere (Williams, 1994) that
creating safety in the therapeutic atmosphere is a special challenge
for abuse survivors and those who work with them, since in many

cases survivors of abuse have found "every 'trustworthy' individual" in their lives to be abusive (p. 165). The therapist's role in creating safety has to do with validation—"The best way the therapist can fulfill her responsibility . . . is by faithfully bearing witness to her [the client's] story" (Herman, 1992, p. 192).

The therapist's role in creating safety has to do with validation.

The facilitator struggled to bring the group to discuss emotional safety as separate from physical safety. Trust emerged as a significant factor. All of the group members stated that they felt they would have been unable to speak in group if they had not been acquainted with the other members:

> **Beth:** I'm the same way [as Charlene]—I just don't say anything—I just listen to what they say [in a new environment] until a couple hours later. [Then] I'll open my mouth. (All nod.)
>
> **Sandra:** Um, does the fact that it's small, there's only three of you and me here—is that helpful? If there were more people here would it be tougher? (All respond simultaneously while nodding affirmatively.)
>
> **Beth:** Um-hmm. (Nods.)
>
> **Catherine:** It would be tougher.
>
> **Charlene:** I don't think I would be able to say anything—I wouldn't feel—I don't think I could—I'd just sit there and freeze.

Significantly, this was the only occasion during the entire experience that group members spoke simultaneously and finished one another's thoughts. Seconds later, this "knowing each other" was defined by the group as trust:

> **Catherine:** You don't know that person [who might attend a therapy group with you].
>
> **Charlene:** You don't know that—you don't know what the other person's thinking.

(Again, all speak simultaneously and complete their statements rather than allow another person to finish.)

Beth: Yeah. Like if that person hates you—

Charlene: Yeah, exactly, Beth. Thank you. I didn't want to say it but—

Catherine: Like if that other person's trustworthy.

Obviously, the ideas of trust and safety in the context of relationship were central concerns for the women. As the facilitator summed up, "So you're saying that knowing each other—even if you don't get along, and I imagine you don't get along all the time—(members smile and nod)—just knowing each other gives you an added piece of trust." (All nod.)

Week Three: Emerging Discomfort

The following week, Sandra initiated discussion about changes that might have occurred since group members shared abuse stories. They expressed increased anger and shortness of temper as well as difficulty sleeping and short-term memory loss. Sandra responded with psychoeducational information related to coping with those types of difficulties. Finally, the topic of confidentiality was reviewed. Beth reported extreme anger with Charlene, as she believed Charlene had broken confidentiality about the group with a staff person from her residence. Group members began a collage homework assignment, to "explain about yourself."

Week Four: Coping

Coping with current emotional discomfort was also the focus of the fourth week. Sandra conducted a lengthy psychoeducational session about cognitive methods for dealing with anger or frustration. For the first time, this session was marked by a feeling of disconnectedness between the members and facilitator. It seemed that the members were lost during parts of the lengthy psychoeducational section. They may have had difficulty tying it to current concerns. Field notes read:

She's losing them and responding by getting louder. . . . This is a tough session. I feel like they are dragging their feet. For the first time, I'm very glad I'm not working [i.e., facilitating the group] today. . . . [Later, during break] Small talk is not flowing well, either. [Group facilitator] is having to bring up each topic.

This was a session in which the group facilitator was attempting to differentiate issues related to emotional safety from issues related to physical safety; one of the reasons for what I perceived as a disconnectedness between facilitator and group members may have been that struggle. The group members had pressing concerns related to physical safety, which they seemed to see as synonymous with emotional safety.

A postgroup interview with the facilitator revealed that another cause for the difficult session may have been stressors at the residences of the group members due to staff changes. The facilitator stated that she had been in contact with residential staff, who seemed preoccupied with staffing changes rather than the emerging emotional discomfort of the group members.

Abuse As Context

The fifth week included discussion of the abuse history in an implied manner: members discussed what they see as current ramifications of their past traumas. Beth stated that her abuse and eventual pregnancy with her brother's child became apparent to her family almost immediately by her deteriorating hygiene and increased temper and alcohol abuse. Eventually, she had an abortion.

Collage assignments were also discussed during this session. The group facilitator instructed members to construct collages of "things that tell us about you. You can add the part about the secret inside you, or you don't have to. . . . Use this to take a look at who you are." For the most part, collages focused on the present, family, and coping skills. Beth's had the word "healthy" in large letters in the center. Catherine's included a picture of herself in costume and wearing a mask; she continued to express anxiety about potentially telling her parents about the abuse experience, an issue she ultimately took up in individual therapy.

The therapeutic process for survivors of childhood sexual abuse
ideally includes a progression from past to present focus.

Herman and Lawrence (1994) have suggested that the group process for adult survivors of childhood sexual abuse ideally includes just such a progression from past to present focus:

> At the point where group members have bonded . . . have a fairly good beginning understanding of the psychological impact [of childhood incest] . . . [they develop] an understanding of how incest manifests itself in the symptoms and problems they face in their current lives. (p. 444)

Ending

The final week of the group experience completed the transition from past to future. A large part of the meeting was focused on concrete current concerns related to the general topic of taking care of physical and emotional needs. For Beth, the concern was the anxiety related to an upcoming mammogram. Catherine's worry was dealing with chest pains she suffered on one or two occasions. Group members began to interact with one another much more extensively than they had prior to this meeting, looking at and speaking to one another. The second half of the session was focused on deciding which characteristics of significant relationships are positive or negative. The work of the group was reviewed, and members stated again that the most positive experience for them was sharing their secrets.

Nonverbal exercises assisted in the identification of relevant emotional issues. For example, the drawing exercise described previously was employed in the first session. Later in the group, the collage assignment played an important role in highlighting the present.

It seems significant that both facilitator and members strove together to keep the group present-focused. Once the initial secrets were revealed, group members seemed to have little inclination to rehash their abuse experiences. Instead, they seemed more interested in discussing present difficulties in the context of the past abuse without making reference to the specific incidents. On at least two occasions, the facilitator asked whether members wanted to discuss their experiences; both times, they asked to "move on."

Both facilitator and members strove together to keep the group present-focused.

The group facilitator also worked to keep the group present-focused. This appeared to be in response to the members' wishes; however, her concern regarding implanting memories and potential "false memory syndrome" led her to steer clear of abuse re-collections on a number of occasions. For example, she had no intention to have members share abuse stories during the first group session. She reminded members that they did not have to discuss uncomfortable feelings or events on a number of occasions, saying repeatedly, "You don't have to talk about details," and "You don't have to talk about what is uncomfortable." This is an example of an unusual style of intervention in work with sexual abuse survivors. However, it has been suggested elsewhere. Williams (1994) reported:

> . . . reliving every single abusive experience is not necessary. . . .
> Remembering, reliving, and reexperiencing enough of the trauma
> to enable the client to recognize the impact of the abuse, diffuse
> its emotional cathexis, and diminish self-blame are all that is
> required. (p. 163)

Finally, group time spent in a very didactic fashion, such as occurred during the fifth session, may have been a way of avoiding spontaneous group conversation. The section that included any re-collections was the period following the midgroup break, and this period was consistently the shortest segment of formal work.

Sandra is very conscious of the current "false memory syndrome" debate. She feels that the potential to do more harm than good to clients is very real, as is the potential for damaging lawsuits. As a result, she screened potential group members very carefully. If a referral source suggested that a potential client did not

ever report abuse—that a sexual abuse history was simply suspected by mental health professionals—that client was considered
ineligible for the group. One client was deemed ineligible due to
discomfort with the idea of participating in groups. During the
group process, Sandra was very careful when discussing re-collections, saying in one postgroup interview, "I'm really struggling not
to lead them," and in another interview, "I'm struggling with not
inserting what they're not saying."

The controversy regarding recovered memories of childhood
sexual abuse permeated every aspect of this treatment group, from
the unusually careful initial screening process to the very structured
treatment itself. Most sessions were highly structured; a great deal
of time was spent in a psychoeducational modality in which members' input was minimal.

---

*Somehow, something about the group atmosphere created a feeling
of safety for the members. Two members discussed their sexual
abuse stories for the first time in their lives.*

The group facilitator was, in fact, wary of the members discussing their abuse histories at all. At no point did she encourage them
to disclose their stories. Despite all this, two members did discuss
their sexual abuse stories for the first time in their lives—in the first
group session. Somehow, something about the group atmosphere
created a feeling of safety for the members. To begin to determine
the components of this atmosphere of safety, the disclosure process
itself must be examined in detail.

Chapter 5

First-Time Stories:
The Interactional Context

> *Stories of therapy do not come only from something that happens "inside" the troubled or even between them, not even something inside and between, but rather they come from all this plus something else that happens between them and the therapist.* (DeShazer, 1994, p. xvii)

This chapter focuses on incidents in which re-collections of childhood sexual abuse were shared by group members. Using the grounded theory approach, a number of interactional strategies emerged. Each was triangulated with at least one additional source, and all hypotheses and conclusions were member-checked with the group facilitator and/or members. In an attempt to consider the data as objectively as possible, no literature was reviewed during the analysis phase, with the exception of a new text on dissociative disorders (Lynn and Rhue, 1994), as the facilitator employed that term in a postgroup interview while discussing her concerns about Catherine. Therefore, the literature reported in the previous chapters comprises the context for the data analysis.

The following *interactional strategies* emerged:

1. Conversation repair
2. Stillness and silence
3. Event transitions
4. Member orientation

The first-time disclosures of sexual abuse re-collections occurred in the context of a number of interactional strategies used by the group facilitator and the group members.

This section examines the first-time disclosure of re-collections of childhood sexual abuse that were shared by Beth and Catherine during the first group session. Particular focus has been placed on the conversational context of the first words of these disclosures, to begin to identify interactional factors that seem to facilitate the initial disclosure.

INTERACTIONAL STRATEGIES

Conversation repair refers to the practice of "jumping in" and assisting a speaker.

Conversation Repair

The "self-righting mechanism" of the organization of language has been referred to as conversation repair in conversation analysis (Schlegoff, Jefferson, and Sacks, 1977, p. 381). As an interactional strategy, conversation repair refers to the practice of "jumping in" and assisting the speaker. This is the type of interaction, for example, when a speaker is searching for a name or a word and a listener (the repairer) supplies a suggestion. Though it is offered under the guise of helpfulness, it is not clear that conversation repair actually facilitates conversation. Instead, it seems to interrupt the flow of the conversation in spite of "helping" the speaker and perhaps shortening a period of conversational silence.

Group members did not interrupt each other. The group interaction had an unusual smoothness.

In informal conversation among nonclinical populations, conversation repair has been found to be initiated by either the speaker or listener (self-correction versus other-correction). Self-correction has been found to be much more common, as well as the more interactionally functional type (Schlegoff, Jefferson, and Sacks, 1977). In addition, it has been suggested that other-initiated conversation repair may function as a mechanism for the labeling of conversants as intellectually handicapped (Leudar, 1989). The interactional strategy of conversation repair, as both self- and other-initiated, emerged as important to the overall group atmosphere early in the analysis of data. The atmosphere of the group sessions was unexpected; the sessions seemed somehow to be unusually orderly, unusually organized. After repeated viewing and listening to the dialogue without watching the interaction, it became evident that members did not interrupt one another or talk over one another as frequently as might be expected. The conversation had a smoothness that seemed unusual. Eventually, it became apparent that very few instances of conversation repair were occurring.

Other-initiated conversation repair, or "jumping in" to assist the speaker, results in a break in the flow of conversation. Again, a speaker may stammer or hesitate in the process of speech while searching for a name or a word to express a thought. If a member of the audience attempts to supply the term for which the speaker is searching, that is an instance of conversation repair. This is not uncommon in everyday speech. However, persons who seem to require frequent conversational assistance are often ultimately considered disabled (Leudar, 1989).

The repair of conversation, then, may be indicative of a powerful or controlling role on the part of the person offering the repair. Given the diagnostic labels carried by the group members as well as the power differential inherent in the therapeutic environment, the term "repair" is employed here to reflect what appears to be a power differential in the employment of this interactional strategy. In light of this issue of conversational power or control, it seemed important to look at the therapy group with an eye toward incidents of conversational repair due to the potential influence of the exercise of power on the creation of the abuse stories. Data were analyzed for occasions of conversation repair by the initiator of the repair (the repairer), the repairee, and the context of the comment. Instances in which the speaker seemed to request assistance, such as by saying " . . . you know?," have not been counted as conversation repair. In addition, statements of reflection by the group facilitator in which she rephrases comments made by participants have not been counted as incidents of conversation repair as they are common to the therapeutic process. Analysis of these speech occurrences was facilitated by listening to the videotape without actually viewing it—incidents of conversation repair are relatively easy to identify in this manner as they may be readily identified as interruptions in the flow of speech.

Note that this perspective on conversation repair may be contrasted to that of aligned speech in joint productions, as outlined by Ferrara (1994) in her sociolinguistic study of individual therapeutic sessions. Defined as "interlocked utterances that are the result of one speaker's initiating a proposition and a second speaker's completing or expanding upon it in a syntactically and semantically consistent manner," joint productions are seen as ways speakers jointly construct verbalizations (p. 146). She does not distinguish between utterances in which the speaker appears to be requesting assistance and those in which the listener provides unsolicited assistance. This perspective is similar to the principle of cooperation as a general guide to conversation as suggested by Grice (cited in Sands, 1988).

Data analysis here seems to support the definition of conversational repair as indicative of a power differential between speakers. Table 5.1 depicts the instances of conversation repair that occurred during the formal work of the group. Instances of conversation repair ranged between one (in session four) to nine (in session two). Session four is the session in which the collage expressive activities were described; group participants spent a relatively large amount of time talking calmly about themselves via the description of their collage assignments.

In total, Catherine supplied twelve of the thirty-two instances of conversation repair, seven times to interrupt Beth's speech and five times during the group facilitator's speech. Beth supplied a comparable fourteen instances of conversation repair, only once during Catherine's speech and thirteen times during the group facilitator's.

TABLE 5.1. Conversation Repair

Session	Time	Repairer	Repairee	Setting
1	0.13.06	C	B	N
	0.15.26	W	B	N
	1.00.26	B	W	R
	1.12.52	B	C	R
2	0.30.49	W	Ch	N
	0.41.56	C	W	N
	0.51.56	Ch	B	N
	0.55.17	B	W	N
	1.19.45	Ch	W	N
	1.29.00	W	Ch	N
	1.36.22	W	Ch	N
	1.39.35	B	W	N
	1.41.54	B	W	N
3	0.25.06	B	W	N
	0.26.33	B	W	N
	0.28.46	C	W	N
	0.30.03	B	W	N
	0.31.16	B	W	N
	0.36.57	B	W	N
	1.40.08	B	W	R
4	0.52.41	B	W	N
5	0.52.17	C	B	N
	2.03.06	C	B	N
	2.05.18	C	B	N
	2.16.51	C	W	N
	2.24.32	B	W	N
6	0.35.09	C	B	N
	0.36.32	C	B	N
	0.38.18	C	B	N
	0.40.36	C	W	N
	0.42.47	B	W	N
	0.51.22	C	W	N

Table Key:

Time: hour. minutes. seconds into group session
W: Worker   C: Catherine   R: During Re-collection
B: Beth   Ch: Charlene   N: Not During Re-collection

Beth's more frequent conversation repair of the facilitator's speech was not unexpected. It has been suggested elsewhere (Gasker, 1991) that persons in residential placements may learn to value and practice interaction with paid staff persons more highly and more often than with peers.

Another factor of importance to Beth's instances of conversation repair is that the majority of them occurred during the third session, directed toward the worker. Five of the six instances occurred during a brief, twelve-minute period in the third session. This was the time when Beth was upset about what she perceived as a break in the group's confidentiality rules by Charlene, who was not present during this session. She appeared to repair the worker's speech frequently in an attempt to facilitate the worker's understanding of the source of her frustration.

Finally, Charlene supplied two instances of conversation repair, once toward Beth and once during the group facilitator's speech. This is in keeping with the relatively short time she spent with the group as well as her overall state of nervousness and inability to discuss issues with the group.

Each of these instances of conversation repair was successful; that is, the initiator of the repair chose a word or phrase that was accepted by the speaker as fitting. In addition, another characteristic of these repairs is that they required only one conversational turn: the repair initiator did not identify the problem and then offer an alternative word or phrase; instead, she simply offered the alternative. Both of these characteristics are different from those found in informal speech among nonclinical populations (Schlegoff, Jefferson, and Sacks, 1977). This may indicate a difference between informal conversation and therapeutic interaction or a difference in interactional organization among clinical and nonclinical populations.

It seems that the low number of instances of conversation repair by the facilitator lent an atmosphere of respect to the group.

Note that the therapist only supplied four instances of conversation repair, and that these occurred during the first two sessions. Three of these instances were directed toward Charlene and one toward Beth. This relatively low number is perhaps a clue about what gave the group an unusual feeling. It seems that this low number of instances of conversation repair by the facilitator lent an atmosphere of respect to the group. The therapist was comfortable with the silence of members as they struggled to express themselves and was willing to wait until they had found what they felt to be the correct word without attempting to efficiently supply it herself. When a group member was struggling to find an appropriate word or phrase, and conversation repair might be expected, the worker occasionally made such supportive comments as, "Take your time."

The therapist was comfortable with the silence of members as they struggled to express themselves.

The setting of all instances of conversation repair seems important in this atmosphere of respect for each individual's storytelling time. Note that of the thirty-two total conversation repairs only three occurred when a member was discussing an abuse re-collection. It appears that the abuse re-collections were especially regarded by the group as times in which a speaker could comfortably keep the floor. Periods of unusual quiet on the part of other group members seemed to mark these re-collection discussions.

STRUCTURAL CONTEXT

Both disclosures occurred in the second half of the first group session, just following the informal break time. The transcription of the initiation of Catherine's disclosure appears on page 63; it was almost forcibly interjected into the group facilitator's plan for the group process. For both Catherine and Beth, the disclosure occurred within the context of their description of a nonverbal drawing exercise in which they were asked to draw a box that might be used to hold something. Both concentrated intensely on the nonverbal exercise for approximately twenty minutes, and both included the first-time re-collection in their descriptions of their drawings.

THE FIRST-TIME STORIES

Catherine's Story

The initial disclosure of Catherine's story began with her attempts to move the group from the break period into the next work phase. To examine closely the group environment surrounding the beginning of this first-time story disclosure, a microanalytic transcription is provided. (See Figure 5.1.)

The transcript depicts a thirty-five-second period of time in which Catherine begins to share her first-time re-collection of childhood sexual abuse. She actually wrote an account of the story along with a drawing during the preceding nonverbal group exercise, so her initial comments as transcribed here are significant. She began by discussing why she has chosen to tell her story for the first time. The verbalizations included during this time are as follows:

> **Therapist:** All right. Umm. You just let me read that and you just let Beth read that—that part that you've never really talked about. Is there anything you can talk about the feelings that are going along with that? You seem like you're kind of worried?
>
> **Catherine:** At this point. Or even scared.
>
> **Therapist:** Tell me what you're scared about, Catherine.
>
> **Catherine:** Elaine [Catherine's sister] finding out that I told you. She told me to keep a secret, which—I can't.

Reading the Transcript

The chart (Figure 5.1) is read from left to right, with Beth's participation along the top third of the chart, Catherine's in the middle, and the group facilitator's along the bottom. This format was chosen to illustrate the verbal and nonverbal group activity as it occurred in real time, with Catherine's activity situated between other members. Essentially, Catherine is surrounded by stillness and silence, despite the presence of other group members.

During this early segment of the interaction, there is some body movement by the group facilitator and the members.

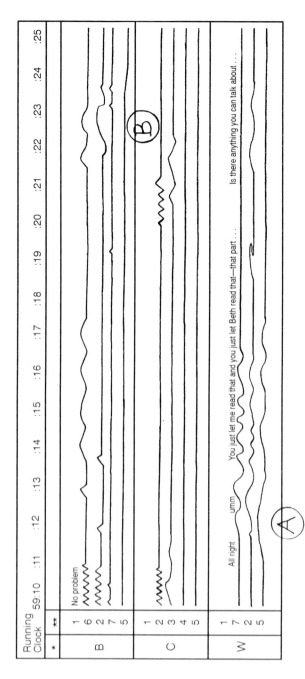

FIGURE 5.1. Initial Disclosure (Part A)

* Group members   ** Communicative elements

B – Beth   1 – verbalizations   4 – hands (clenched)   7 – right hand gestures
C – Catherine   2 – head motion   5 – shoulder movement
W – Worker   3 – right foot tap   6 – facial movement

77

FIGURE 5.1 (Part B)

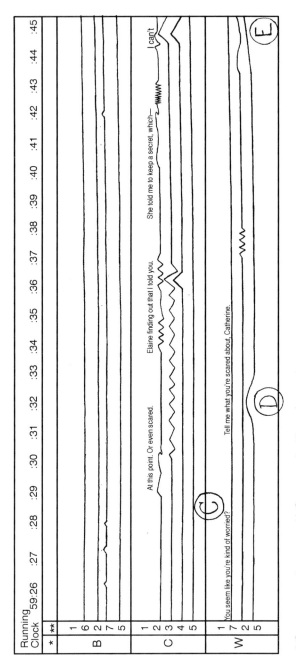

* Group members

B – Beth
C – Catherine
W – Worker

** Communicative elements

1 – verbalizations
2 – head motion
3 – right foot tap

4 – hands (clenched)
5 – shoulder movement
6 – facial movement

7 – right hand gestures

Point A. Note the capital letter A in the bottom left of the chart. This serves to identify a point in time (around 59 minutes and 13 seconds into the group) in which the worker is taking control of the group process. Her head and shoulder movements here are relatively obvious and serve to mark the beginning of a new conversational routine, that of Catherine's verbal description of her nonverbal exercise. Note that during this early segment of the interaction, there is some body movement by the worker and Beth.

Point B. The letter B, located at the transcription of Beth's communicative participation, occurs 59 minutes and 22 seconds into the group experience. Note that a relatively large movement of her head occurred here, followed by an extended period of no discernible movement at all. At this time, just as the worker said, "Is there anything you can talk about the feelings . . . ," Beth turned her head to face Catherine. Because she turned her head and not her shoulders, the position was awkward. Beth was facing straight ahead but looking off to her left at Catherine. She held that uncomfortable pose without moving, apparently without breathing, for the duration of the interaction.

When Catherine begins to speak, the movements of the other group members virtually disappear.

Point C. The letter C (at 59:30) indicates the point at which Catherine begins to speak. This is the first time she is communicating verbally about the incident of sexual abuse, and all group members are aware that she is discussing that topic. Note the increase in Catherine's own body movements: her foot begins tapping rapidly, she gestures with her clenched hands, her head is shaking, and she makes some relatively large shoulder movements. These motions are probably indicative of her own discomfort. However, other group members respond differently. Note that when Catherine begins to speak the movements of the other group members virtually disappear. This is quite unusual in interactional settings. People are constantly in some motion when communicating—nodding, swaying, making pointed gestures. Here, however, the other group members did not even appear to express the small head and shoulder movement usually consistent with breathing. In fact, they appeared to be literally holding their breaths. The possible interactional function of this unusual stillness and silence will be considered in the next chapter.

Points D and E. Letters D and E simply mark a very slight forward movement by the worker. She is leaning forward, almost imperceptibly, toward Catherine. This communicative element probably served to indicate to Catherine that the worker was encouraging her to continue speaking. This small gesture may show the worker's validation of the narrator of this first-time re-collection. She accepted the narrator's need to tell the story and did not press for details. Her slight forward movement, however, served to indicate interest and acceptance. She concluded the brief story with the following validating statement:

> **Therapist:** So when I said to draw a picture of the box, you drew the whole box. You drew what was inside it.
> **Catherine:** (Nods.)
> **Therapist:** I appreciate you telling us with your picture—do you want to tell us anything else?
> **Catherine:** No.
> **Therapist:** Okay.

Beth's Story

Beth's initial disclosure of her re-collection of childhood sexual abuse occurred just five minutes after Catherine's. Her words, as she began to describe her drawing, are not about what she drew, but what she "failed" to draw. The transcription is expanded below:

> **Worker:** How about you, Beth? Tell us a little about your storage box.
> **Beth:** Umm—I didn't put my brother in here, though.
> **Worker:** I'm sorry?
> **Beth:** My brother. My youngest brother. Larry. Umm. I never told my mom or my dad—he wanted to have sex with me. I was like late in my teenagers—age. And I'm afraid if if he was gonna hit me, or do somethin', and—I just failed to put that down on the

paper also. And I lived with my stepmother. And I was very angry and I wanted him to stop it and everything and I didn't know how to go with it, and I got angry with my mom and my dad and myself. I never told anybody about it. And I thought of it and I thought of it and it makes me more angry.

Several characteristics of Beth's verbalization are important. First, her difficulty in articulating emotional issues is apparent, e.g., "I was like late in my teenagers—age." Second, note her unusual interjection of a more formal style of language ("I just failed to put that down on the paper also . . ."), which may be an effective interactional strategy for ensuring that listeners recognize the importance of a statement. Finally, notice her switch to present tense ("I'm afraid if if he was gonna hit me"). This may indicate the intensity of the re-collection or perhaps that she perceives herself to be reliving the experience as she relates it.

Again, the speaker is surrounded by an atmosphere of stillness and silence.

Reading the Transcript

See Figure 5.2 for a depiction of the interactional environment of Beth's first-time re-collection. Note that again the speaker is surrounded by stillness and silence. Once again, the group facilitator assisted in the creation of an atmosphere of validation by not questioning the validity of the first-time re-collection and by respecting the narrator's choice not to divulge specific details of the story.

Point A. At point A in the transcript, the beginnings of another form of validation by the worker may be observed. As she requests that Beth begin to describe her drawing, the worker leans forward, then pulls her chair toward Beth.

Point B. As the worker is completing her forward movement, around the eighth second into the interaction, an interruption occurs. Catherine, who has just finished her first-time re-collection, audibly blows her nose. Beth had begun to speak, and the noise

FIGURE 5.2. Transcription of Beth's Re-Collection (Part A)

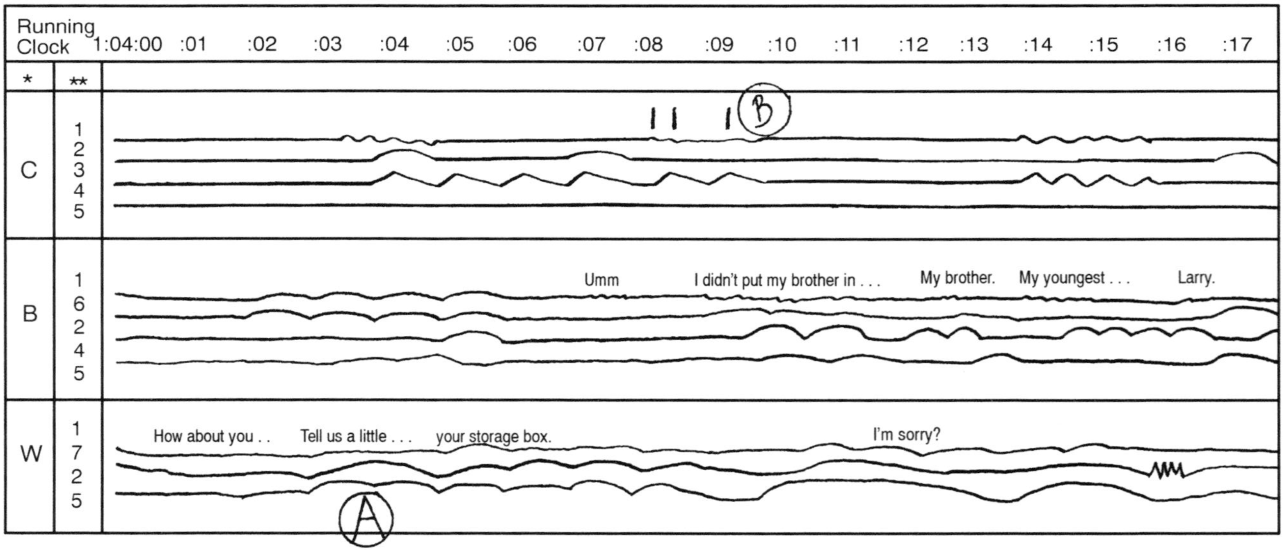

* Group members

B – Beth
C – Catherine
W – Worker

** Communicative elements

1 – verbalizations
2 – head motion
3 – right foot tap

4 – hands (clenched)
5 – shoulder movement
6 – facial movement

7 – right hand gestures

FIGURE 5.2 (Part B)

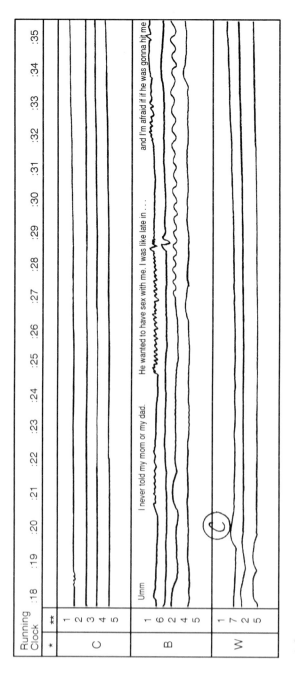

* Group members

B – Beth
C – Catherine
W – Worker

** Communicative elements

1 – verbalizations
2 – head motion
3 – right foot tap

4 – hands (clenched)
5 – shoulder movement
6 – facial movement

7 – right hand gestures

made her words inaudible. The worker asks her to repeat her words with the phrase "I'm sorry," simultaneously apologizing for not being able to hear.

. . . they seem to be completely still and totally attentive to the story that is being told.

Point C. At point C, the validating gesture is completed. The worker folds her hands as they are extended toward Beth. At this point, she settles into an attentive, forward-oriented listening posture. She is hunched over, with her elbows on her knees and hands extended toward Beth. Here both Catherine and the worker begin a period of stillness and silence in which they seem to be completely still and totally attentive to the story that is being told. The only other movement during the interaction occurs when the worker briefly nods to acknowledge the speaker's self-correction of the word "teenage."

TRIANGULATION INTERVIEWS

Triangulation interviews supported the idea that a group may be the vehicle that supports first-time re-collection as well as the suggestion that group members somehow collaborate in making an environment that feels safe enough for first-time re-collections to be shared. On the other hand, the experience of the therapists interviewed differed from those of the observed group in an important way: they were all concerned with when and how to stop the past-focused stories of abuse, which they found could spread within the group to create a problematic negative focus. "It's hard to know when to stop them from ventilating and obsessing over the abuse," one group worker commented.

They felt the greatest benefit of the group was to share these stories that they had never told before.

Members' Perceptions

In interviews following the second and fifth group sessions, as well as in the postgroup interviews, both Beth and Catherine were asked to comment on their first-time re-collections. Both stressed that they felt the greatest benefit of the group was to share these stories they had never told before.

Beth, in particular, articulated her belief that telling the story was a necessary prerequisite to emotional health. Both she and Catherine stressed feeling "safe" and "trusting" in the group atmosphere. When asked pointedly what may have made them feel they could trust the group facilitator and what made them feel safe within the group setting, however, neither had any insights. The following material is an attempt to identify conversational strategies that may have contributed to those feelings of safety and trust.

Stillness and Silence

One of the challenges of the ongoing data analysis process was to identify the communicative elements of the periods of unusual quiet that seemed to mark re-collection discussions. The stillness theme that eventually emerged indicates a period in which there are no verbalizations and little or no movement by audience members. It is the marked absence of movement that seems significant. The period of stillness is difficult to observe on videotape without physically counting seconds; however, it is quite obvious when participating in the group process. The period of stillness lends a feeling of expectation; it is what is commonly called the "pregnant pause." Periods of stillness and silence seemed to accompany re-collections within the group. Thus, when one group member was relating an abuse story, other members became silent and almost entirely motionless.

When one group member was relating an abuse story, the others were both silent and motionless . . . almost to the point of not breathing.

To illustrate, consider the microanalytic transcriptions of two separate speech events occurring during the group process (see

Figures 5.1 and 5.3). The two speech events are similar in a number of ways: both are exactly thirty-five seconds long; both are events in which Catherine is explaining her experiential drawing exercise to the group. A significant difference is that the first event consists of a first-time re-collection of an abuse experience while the second does not.

Contextual Analysis

Figure 5.3 depicts an interaction in the fifth group session in which Catherine has been discussing her concerns about a relative's lack of parenting skills. This issue is tied to her abuse re-collections in two ways: first, she has said that the "bad example" set for her by the perpetrator of the abuse led her to be promiscuous for some time; and second, she has been cautioned by her sister not to have children due to the emotional instability Catherine also perceives to be a result of the abuse. She is discussing her decision not to have children in the interaction in Figure 5.3. The dialogue alone is transcribed below:

> **Therapist:** What-what-what were you trying to tell us here? With this picture?
>
> **Catherine:** Like, usually my sister Mary tells me—not to get married and not to have a child—and I'm just doing the right thing.

Here the narrative is focused on the present. While the past abuse re-collections are directly tied to the conversation, they are not central. Instead, the re-collections form the backdrop for the inter-action. The level of movement surrounding the narrator is decidedly different from that which surrounds her during her first-time recol-lection (Figure 5.1). Here there is considerable movement by both the worker and the other group member.

This type of group quiet and unusual stillness has been experi-enced in intensive outpatient groups as well. When asked if group members "jump in" and help one another tell their stories, the two group facilitators independently said during triangulation inter-views that they were sure they did not. One stated, "No, they sit very quietly and listen. . . . Survivors want to hear other people's stories" (A. Pierre, personal communication, April 13, 1995).

FIGURE 5.3. Catherine's Re-Collections in the Context of Present Life Events (Part A)

* Group members   **** Communicative elements**

B – Beth   1 – verbalizations   4 – hands (clenched)   7 – right hand gestures
C – Catherine   2 – head motion   5 – shoulder movement
W – Worker   3 – right foot tap   6 – facial movement

FIGURE 5.3 (Part B)

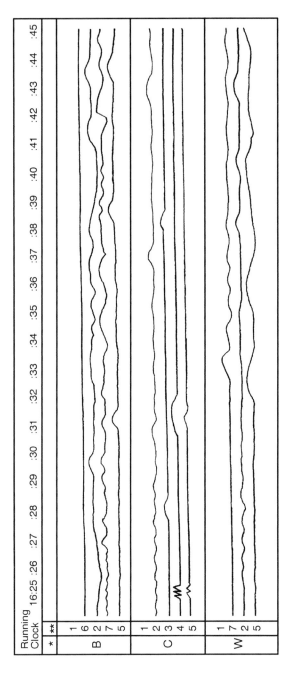

* Group members   ** Communicative elements

B – Beth   1 – verbalizations   4 – hands (clenched)   7 – right hand gestures
C – Catherine   2 – head motion   5 – shoulder movement
W – Worker   3 – right foot tap   6 – facial movement

Such conversational silence is unlike what is usually experienced in day-to-day conversation. It has been suggested that the normal turn-taking mechanism of conversation includes a conversational feature of "at least one at a time" (Schlegoff and Sacks, 1974, p. 236). That is, in informal conversation in a nonclinical setting, speakers notice silence and assign the silence to the speaker whose "turn" it is. That person is then expected to fill the silence, which is experienced as uncomfortable by the other conversationalists.

It is as if no one is in a terrible hurry, as if everyone's story is important.

Taken together, the theme of stillness and silence along with the lack of conversational repair contribute to what feels like a unique social atmosphere. It is as if no one is in a terrible hurry, that every individual's story is important while she tells it. When the collage exercise was completed at the end of the fifth session, movement was minimal but relatively normal, as seen in Figure 5.3. No one, however, had been interrupted in her explanation of how several pages of collage was an expression of her identity. Field notes from that point in the session read, "Note: Very calm feeling in the room now."

Event Transitions

This category refers to the boundary between conversational routines. These boundaries are typically marked by kinesic changes, along with alterations in voice characteristics (Erickson, 1992a). For example, when the group facilitator ended the pregroup social time, she would typically say something such as, "Well, I guess we might as well get started." At that time, there would be a change in body orientation and focus of attention as group members shifted to the new communication event. These event transitions may be observed in practically all communication events. They have been determined to be of special importance to this group experience, however. The importance of event transitions emerged from a repeated viewing of the segment of tape one that has been transcribed in Figure 5.1. During this segment, something unusual was occurring, in that Catherine was managing to have her agenda put on the table, so to speak. Up to that point, the facilitator had been initiating each transition. At that point, Catherine verbally and behaviorally "insisted" that her concerns be heard. She accomplished this through interjecting her statements into the conversation at every opportunity, in a manner that would have been considered quite inappropriate in any other setting in this culture.

The complete verbal transcript of Catherine's unsolicited efforts to discuss a re-collection of sexual abuse has been presented in the previous chapter. The communication event occurred during the first group session, just four minutes after Sandra had facilitated a transition to the midgroup break. During the first several minutes of break, group members and participants got up for a snack and hot drink. They spoke briefly while standing, then returned to their group seats for the remainder of the break period. Beth initiated small talk with Sandra, then with Catherine. Catherine then abruptly shifted the topic in an attempt to facilitate a transition back to the official work of the group.

The person who facilitates event transitions holds a powerful position.

The person who facilitates event transitions holds a powerful position. She is able to govern the topic and the tone of the conversation that follows. The group facilitator dictated all of the other transitions throughout the group experience. This is perhaps not unusual, since it is the group facilitator's role to control the therapeutic process, that is, to consciously use the aspects of beginnings, middles, and endings to the benefit of the therapy participants (Smalley, 1967). Likewise, Ferrara (1994) has pointed out that "in therapeutic discourse it is the therapist who attends to the role of framing the discourse" (p. 42). However, it also might indicate the facilitator's need or desire to dictate the conversational limits. In some cases, this could be functional, in that the group would be assisted in retaining focus and staying on task. In others, however, it could be a dysfunctional way of avoiding taboo areas or discussing only those topics on the facilitator's agenda.

Orientation

The orientation theme indicates the physical orientation of group members, referring to the direction they appear to be focusing their attention. In some cases, the direction of the front of the body appears significant; in others, the movement of face or eyes appears to be different from that of the rest of the body. Another component of orientation may be the front-to-back movement of the torso as an expression of interest in a particular speaker or speech event.

It was difficult to determine the meaning of the orientation of these group members in this setting. For the most part, members addressed comments to the facilitator and simultaneously made eye contact with her. When one group member was speaking, other members generally oriented in her direction, with the facilitator often leaning toward the speaker. An exception to this fairly consistent orientation interaction was Catherine's orientation during some occasions when other group members were speaking. She kept her face directed away from the speaker and toward the facilitator, but shifted her gaze toward the speaker. In this way, the speaker could not tell whether she was being observed. This clandestine observation did not seem to occur during any specific group activities or topic discussions. It is not readily seen on the videotaped recording, but was observed by both the researcher and the group facilitator during sessions. Interestingly, Beth commented during the follow-up interview that she attempts to show persons with whom she is speaking that she is being attentive by consciously making eye contact. When asked specifically what aspects of the group were important, members made no comments about orientation. Lacking member insights into the importance of orientation as well as having a limited number of group members makes any generalization regarding the role orientation may play in the group process difficult.

This is in direct contrast to the suggestion made by Ferrara (1994) that retellings of narratives in therapy may be universally characterized as "therapeutic" and indicative of "continuing growth of awareness" (p. 53). Ferrara's view is based on the notion suggested by therapists that retellings of personal narratives in the therapeutic setting allow clients to note the importance of the event, to become aware of its emotional impact, and finally to come to experience the affect. It is not uncommon for therapists to believe, as Ferrara's sources did, that retellings of personal narratives need to be repeated until the telling includes an emotional component. That is, therapists often believe that if "storytelling in therapy becomes too ritualized, too pat, the therapist feels that progress is not being made" (Ferrara, 1994, p. 53). This belief would consequently lead to attempts by therapists to elicit repeated retellings of personal narratives as stories about the past in order to allow the expected (read "appropriate") affective component to emerge.

Repeated tellings of traumatic stories until they include emotional content is not necessary. What is more important is the time orientation of the story. A focus on the present indicates a healthy movement out of the past.

The findings here suggest that not only are these repeated retellings unnecessary they may be antithetical to therapeutic process. What appears to be significant is not whether an emotive component is included in a personal narrative but rather the narrative's orientation to past or present. The women who shared first-time re-collections in this group stated repeatedly and emphatically in follow-up interviews that the most important benefit of the group was the sharing of their stories. Still, they chose not to reiterate the stories in the context of disclosing past events once the initial disclosure was made. Even when explicitly given the opportunity, they asked that the group "move on."

CLINICAL TECHNIQUES

Chapter 6

Therapeutic Implications

We have seen that the question of truth or falsity is all but irrelevant to the concerns of adults struggling with issues related to recollections of childhood sexual abuse. The issue has become an emotional debate in the popular press and in the scientific media. This emotional debate has divided professionals and laypersons alike. As Schwartz (1969) has suggested, when the polarization of controversial issues enters the professional arena, these polarizations present obstacles to the development of professional knowledge:

> They may serve for a while to dramatize important issues, but the banner-waving, the quarrels over abstractions, and the ritualistic emphasis on goals without means, all impede the work on the central professional tasks. (p. 84)

The central task here is helping. Instead of participating in the so-called "false memory" debate, mental health practitioners can best assist clients who bear re-collections of sexual trauma by stepping back from the dichotomous thinking that characterizes the discussion.

To repeat, the central task for the helping professional is helping. From this perspective, the practitioner must approach adult disclosures of childhood sexual abuse in another way—by viewing such re-collections as life narratives that are extremely difficult to share with others. This places the therapeutic focus on the initial telling of a re-collection.

The questions then facing the therapist are the following:

- How do I create a helping environment that feels safe enough for clients to disclose first-time stories of childhood sexual abuse?
- How do I create this environment without making that disclosure an agenda for clients for whom it is not relevant?

- How do I respond to the disclosure when it happens? Can I be supportive without joining too much with the client's pain?
- What do I do if I really don't believe the story?

The answer to these questions begins with a discussion of a broad theoretical perspective. In this perspective, the first-time disclosure is viewed as a beginning part of the life narrative, a "rough draft" of a life story being told for the first time. This chapter provides a discussion of the therapeutic implications of this approach to disclosures of sexual abuse. These implications are basic perspectives that will color a therapist's clinical practice in a general way. More specific therapeutic guidelines are provided in the following chapters.

In this chapter, the therapeutic perspectives discussed include the following: the disclosure of childhood trauma as a life narrative; the function of therapist nonaction in the helping environment; and the importance of conversational repair and event transitions in the successful therapy process.

A practitioner's theory is the story he or she brings to the therapeutic setting.

TRAUMATIC STORIES AS LIFE NARRATIVES

Narrative is a useful metaphor for allowing practitioners to understand the way clients make meaning. It provides a vehicle for incorporating a constructivist perspective into theory and practice, as well as holding potential as a vehicle for explaining the way in which culture, social and psychological theory, and individual stories intersect. For example, culture maintains meanings and represents them through stories and nonverbal expression, while a practitioner's theory is the story he or she brings to the helping process. Clients may be assisted in formulating functional life narratives with the therapist as catalyst. Eventually, the themes of these stories may be projected back into the culture, and the stories of vulnerable populations may be given a positive voice in the politics of cultural meaning-making (Saleebey, 1994). This is the postmodern response to a rapidly shifting social scene: the assumption that people live in a myriad of worlds in their daily lives and must call upon a myriad of selves to navigate those worlds.

Narrative Theory in Practice

The basic perspective outlined in this chapter has been drawn from original research conducted by the author with clients from her own clinical practice as well as the clinical practice of others. A discussion of these research methods is provided in the Appendix. Some of the other, more specific, techniques included in the following chapters have been gleaned from the generous input of workshop participants who were willing to share their ideas and uncertainties among colleagues. Finally, some techniques have been developed as a logical extension of the theory provided here and are deemed successful based only on the limited practice of a few clinicians. They are offered as suggestions only and should be used with discretion under the consultation or supervision of a qualified professional.

Story Validation

In narrative therapy related to first-time disclosures of abuse, the most significant basic perspective is to recognize the importance of validation. In one sense, validation refers to the therapist's willingness to allow the client to present a perspective that may not seem credible. The narrator (an appealing synonym for "client") may describe his or her experience in a manner very different from the way other participants would describe the same event.

Ways to Validate a Client/Narrator's Story:

- *Allow the client to present a perspective that may not seem credible*
- *Do not question the validity of the story*
- *Respect a client's choice to divulge few (or many) details about the incident*

A therapist might validate a narrator's choice of description in two ways: by not questioning its validity and by respecting a narrator's choice not to divulge details regarding an incident. In addition, the helper may validate the narrative by accepting the identity that it depicts (Sands, 1996).

First-time stories place the narrator in a vulnerable position. It is appropriate that they are allowed to be told with no changes, or "narrative repair."

First-Time Stories

In general, narrative therapy progresses quickly from validation to editing, or narrative repair. However, the notion of therapeutic narrative repair is incomplete, particularly when considered relative to situations in which clients are constructing re-collections of childhood sexual abuse. When a therapist is confronted with a life story related to childhood sexual abuse, it is likely that the story is being verbalized for the very first time. This timing issue takes on a great deal of significance for the storyteller, who is vulnerable in terms of trust and who is seeking a safe environment in which to try out an initial telling of the story. Here validation without *any* form of repair is appropriate.

Narrative smoothing can be an insidious way of stifling the client's voice.

Spence has recently cautioned against the "narrative smoothing" which may characterize therapeutic listening to stories that seem to lack credibility (1994, p. 221). In narrative smoothing, the therapist attempts to interpret the story in a way that selects certain aspects of the story and edits out others. This process of smoothing, a kind of heavy-handed story editing, essentially superimposes the therapist's standards of believability onto the story under the guise of theoretical interpretation. In a second type of narrative smoothing, the therapist may even directly confirm or disconfirm stories as they are told, through interpretation or leading questions.

For example, one therapist listened to a young Hispanic man tell a first-time story of engaging in what he believed to be a consenting sexual relationship with an older woman. He had recently come to wonder whether the relationship had been abusive; he had been thirteen at the time, while his partner was significantly older. At the time of the disclosure, the young man was concerned about the child he knew he had fathered as a result of the relationship. For that reason, he was struggling with his definition of the incident. During his first-time disclosure, the therapist almost immediately insisted upon referring to the experience as "statutory rape," as a way of helping the client recognize both the inappropriateness of the older woman's behavior and his inability to provide consent at such a young age. The problem with the intervention was that it glossed over the client's own emotional experience; it served to edit the client's life story without his own input as author, and it made him uncomfortable with the disclosure in general. Later, the client stated that he felt compelled to defend the woman, rather than to focus on his own emotional experience in the past and present.

Obviously, narrative smoothing can be an insidious way of stifling the client's voice. If a client is expressing a story of childhood sexual abuse for the first time, narrative smoothing may be perceived as invalidating. When a client and therapist are struggling to create an environment of trust, invalidation of a newborn story could be disastrous to the developing relationship. Spence (1994) has proposed that the therapist be especially open to the first-time story, to keep in mind that it is emerging as it is told, to consider its hermeneutic value. He has referred to this type of listening as paying attention to the "context of discovery" (p. 229).

In other words, the context of discovery perspective asks the therapist to wonder about why the client is telling the story at this particular time, to wonder why he or she is telling it in this particular way. The context of discovery is a concern about the function of the first-time disclosure.

Diagnostic Wondering

Don't ask:
  Could this story possibly be true?

Do ask:
  Why is the client telling this story at this particular time?
  Why is he or she telling it in this particular way?

A client's emerging story is a fragile extension of himself or herself. This hopeful new narrator is creating, perhaps for the first time, a re-collection by which he or she hopes to define "self." For an adult who defines himself or herself as a survivor of childhood sexual abuse, the risks involved in the telling may be tremendous. A therapist is called upon to validate the story—to consider its newness and allow some latitude in gauging its credibility, to accept the emerging definition of self the client is postulating via the story, and to respect the storyteller's choice to leave out certain details.

Validation supports the client in the risk-taking, trust-testing endeavor that is the first-time disclosure.

Validation serves to lay the groundwork for future narrative therapy, or narrative repair. It functions to reinforce the initial task of verbalizing the life story. It supports the client in the risk-taking, trust-testing endeavor that is the initial disclosure of a painful re-collection. Most important, validation allows the client to perceive his or her own agency in the story creation. With validation, the client can recognize "self" as creator, not creature.

Validation allows the client to perceive his or her own agency in the story creation. With validation, the client can recognize "self" as creator, not creature.

Authorship, Ownership

Chances are, a re-collection of childhood sexual abuse is one in which the client has played a role in someone else's story. Because he or she has felt unable to share this story, the client has continued in this passive role along with a corresponding sense of powerlessness. The mere telling of the story in a safe, validating environment is the first step toward recognition of ownership, authorship, agency. This first-time story is a client's initial attempt to use his or her own voice. In the context of the telling of a painful re-collection, the client may be hearing his or her voice for the first time.

> *In the context of the first-time telling of a painful re-collection, the
> client may be hearing his or her own voice for the first time.*

Validating, Not Investigating

It is clear that validation is an important part of integrating re-collections into the life story, particularly in a manner consistent with a
positive self-image. For the first-time re-collection, validation is particularly important. Participants in this study stated over and over again
that the most important benefit they received from their participation in
therapy was their ability to tell their stories.

Narrative psychologists Singer and Salovey (1993) have suggested that negative, self-defining memories are organized around
some unresolved conflict. Seeking to master the conflict, individuals return consciously or unconsciously to the unpleasant self-defining memories: "Only by reviving the memories into consciousness
do individuals avail themselves of an opportunity to recast the
meaning of previous events or to re-imagine them in a way that is
more palatable to their self-image" (p. 41). On the other hand, they
caution that "it is important for therapists to be mindful of the
possibility that they may elicit memories from their clients that
confirm their own hypotheses" (p. 186). Their work is supportive
of what has been observed in this study. Therapists must be willing
to allow their clients to share abuse re-collections while avoiding
their amplification and potential detrimental consequences in the
therapeutic setting.

The initial disclosure of a childhood sexual abuse re-collection is
a first-time story. As such, it requires validation. The telling of a
credible story may be far down the road. The telling of a functional,
behaviorally adaptive story may be far down the road as well. But
the telling itself is the first step. There is likely to be no place for
narrative repair in that first step.

> *To stop at validation is to stop an unfinished therapeutic process.*

It is critical, however, to note that validation is just that—a first step in narrative therapy. In a therapist's zeal to create a safe environment for the telling of life stories, validation may take on disproportionate importance. To stop at validation is to stop an unfinished therapeutic process. When no repair, or editing, is conducted with an unbelievable or dysfunctional story, the client may be set up to take on a role as an extreme dependent in the creation of his or her story. He or she must rely on a small number of believers—perhaps fellow victims or perhaps the therapist alone—with whom to share the story. The goal is to integrate this first-time story into the rest of the client's life narrative in a functional way that supports a developing understanding of the self. The client must do that in concert with others. Eventually, narrative repair is necessary and will become a focus of the developing therapeutic milieu. But first, the all-important initial disclosure must be facilitated in the helping environment.

To Believe or Not To Believe

The therapist need not commit to a stance of believer or nonbeliever. He or she does not have to enter such a debate in the context of a helping relationship because it is not relevant to the client's progress. Validating emotions is not the same as agreeing to an objective perception of reality.

---

*On rare occasions, a client will ask some version of this point-blank question: "**Do you believe me?**"*

On rare occasions, a client will ask some version of this point-blank question: "Do you believe me?" It is best not to respond to this sort of query with a show of nervousness and insecurity by the therapist. A lack of self-confidence in one's own beliefs and values will hardly engender a client's confidence in the therapeutic process. Instead, this question of belief can be used as a springboard into the heart of the therapeutic issue—the client's ability to recognize that he or she is the author of the story. What could be a more powerful therapeutic intervention than to help clients realize that the way they understand their life experiences is entirely in their own control?

A sensible answer to the question "Do you believe me?" is "I wish that wouldn't be important to you." The therapist's role is to validate the emotions and empower the client to realize that the story is his or her own creation. In fact, the idea of therapists assisting clients to recognize that they are the authors of their life stories and helping them to recognize their power in using their stories to think about themselves and their relationships differently is beginning to be suggested in the literature of the helping professions (Germain, 1990; Laird, 1989; Reissman, 1989).

A sensible answer to the question "Do you believe me?" is **"I wish that wouldn't be important to you."**

Once they are viewed as re-collections or life narratives, stories about childhood sexual abuse are no longer horrific, painful tales that explain current life problems. Instead, even the most painful re-collections may become vehicles for personal growth and can be tools for assisting their narrators to change their identities from those of victims to those of survivors.

THERAPIST NONACTION

This section describes what is perhaps the most difficult intervention a therapist can provide in the clinical setting. It describes a perspective in which the most valued action by the clinician is to do absolutely nothing. Doing nothing—even purposefully—is unspeakably difficult for the helping professional.

Therapist nonaction is perhaps the most difficult intervention to conduct.

Therapists are helpers. We have a long history in our personal and professional lives of being sensitive to the pain of others. We feel their emotional discomfort, and we reach out to help. Therefore, it takes a great deal of patience and practice to master the therapeutic art of nonaction. In the therapeutic setting, nonaction means maintaining both stillness and silence, two most unusual therapeutic activities.

No Communication: A Powerful Statement

Without the components of stillness and silence, there would be no first-time disclosure of childhood sexual abuse. The therapist must provide an atmosphere of safety, in which clients' abuse stories are respected and validated. For participants in this research, stillness and silence appeared to be necessary elements in the facilitation of the initial disclosure process. It has been noted elsewhere that self-help groups for incest survivors often exploit the benefits of silence with what is called a "no cross-talk rule," in which members are not allowed to interrupt one another's speech at all (Herman and Lawrence, 1994, p. 450). However, these authors have contrasted the "no cross-talk" approach of self-help groups with the interactional approach of professionally facilitated groups, in which members' interaction with one another is encouraged and analyzed (Herman and Lawrence, 1994).

It is proposed here that all groups (two or more people in conversation) are interactional to some degree. Thus, a therapist might work to capitalize on the characteristics of stillness and silence in order to facilitate disclosure while being cognizant of the nonverbal aspects of communication as well. These communicative elements may also be profited by and analyzed for the benefit of the therapy participants, whether in individual or group process.

Finally, after an agonizing (at least for the therapist*) twenty-nine consecutive seconds of absolute stillness and silence . . . the first-time disclosure emerged.*

A worker's stillness and silence has been demonstrated to be a significant factor in the first-time abuse disclosure of an individual client as well as in the group setting (Gasker and Tebb, 1995). In the individual therapy session described in that study, the therapist and client strove for most of the session to create an atmosphere conducive to the discussion of the difficult topic of an incestuous experience. Finally, after an agonizing (at least for the therapist) period of twenty-nine consecutive seconds of absolute stillness and silence, the first-time disclosure finally emerged.

Try sometime to maintain silence in an informal conversation for an extended period of time. You will quickly discover that most people become uncomfortable in just a few seconds. First, they begin to fidget, the discomfort in the room becomes almost palpable, and finally someone blurts out some verbalization—often a frustrated shout!

Most therapists find it nearly unbearable not to "rescue" the client from the discomfort that results from conversational silence.

Helping professionals in particular seem to find the maintenance of conversational silence difficult. In the helping environment especially, most therapists find it nearly unbearable not to "rescue" the client from the discomfort that results from conversational silence. Both stillness and silence, however, must be practiced and cultivated by a therapist who wishes to allow a client's own story to emerge in a session. It is imperative that therapists adopt the perspective in which stillness and silence is recognized as a valued intervention. Saying nothing is perhaps the most powerful statement a therapist can make.

CONTROLLING THE PROCESS

A therapist who is cognizant of the communicative elements that mark conversational transitions will be able to make the most of those transitions. In this way, he or she keeps the therapy focused while recognizing that urgent communication needs might manifest themselves in attempts on the part of clients to control the process.

For example, social processes of all kinds typically include a beginning, a middle, and an end. These sections of any interaction are usually controlled and maintained by all of the participants acting in concert. Let's say a group of friends enter a casual restaurant and find a seat. A good waiter or waitress will approach the table quickly and make some sort of very brief casual conversation. After the small talk, someone in the group is likely to move around a bit and shift slightly in the seat. This slight movement marks the end of the first stage of the interaction.

Typically, that tiny fidget cues the waiter or waitress to take a beverage order. Suddenly, the diners are engaged in the middle part of the eating experience—the real purpose of the encounter. They state their wishes and the server is off to get their drinks. When the beverages are served a few moments later, the diners close their menus to signal that they are ready to order. Or, an involved conversation at the table tells the experienced server to pause before approaching the table and asking for the order. He or she knows that a bigger tip awaits the server who is able to read the diners' wishes from their actions. If the approach is too hasty, the diners may feel the server is intrusive. If the server waits too long, the diners quickly become impatient and the tip reflects their impatience. The same type of process will signal when the diners are ready for their check.

A client who appears to be "rudely" putting his or her story forward at an "inappropriate" time may simply be demonstrating a sense of urgency . . .

This type of complicated interactional communication occurs nonverbally in almost every social setting. It is not consciously intentional, but it is quite purposeful. In therapy as well as in the restaurant business, its benefits can be used to advantage. A therapist whose perspective includes an understanding of these aspects of social process will recognize conversational elements that are unusual and ordinarily seen as socially unacceptable. That is, a client who appears to be "rudely" putting his or her story forward at an "inappropriate" time in the therapeutic process might simply be demonstrating the urgency he or she feels about the telling. As in the example provided in the previous chapter, a therapist cognizant of event transitions and sensitive to client needs will be flexible in allowing clients to control the therapeutic process when a first-time story might be involved. In the same way, the classic "doorknob" comment* need not be viewed as a form of resistance; it may well be a very functional way for a client to state a first-time story in a manner that will not be altered by the therapist.

Therapeutic Guidelines for Client-Centered Practice:

1. *Understand the need for clients to occasionally control the social process of therapy*
2. *Appreciate the importance of therapist nonaction*
3. *View first-time disclosures of traumatic re-collections as "rough drafts" of an emerging life story*

These perspectives—understanding the need for clients to occasionally control the social process of therapy; appreciating the importance of therapist nonaction; and viewing disclosures of childhood sexual abuse as beginning, unpolished life narratives—provide a foundation for informed practice with adults who may have traumatic childhood stories to tell. This foundation supports a client-centered practice in which the client authors his or her own life story.

In this way, client's stories are not infused with therapist's values, and clients begin to recognize their own power in creating and maintaining their own shifting life narratives. Ultimately, clients shift their own self-images from those of sexual abuse victims to those of sexual abuse survivors.

In addition to the general foundation for practice discussed previously, the following chapters will focus on specific therapeutic guidelines. These guidelines serve the purpose of creating the kind of therapeutic environment that facilitates first-time adult disclosures of childhood sexual abuse. In addition, the following chapters discuss the therapeutic management of these disclosures beginning with the dramatic first moment of the telling. The goal is the creation of a safe environment before, during, and after the disclosure takes place.

---

*An important issue that a client introduces at the very end of a session—with a hand on the doorknob.

Chapter 7

Therapeutic Techniques

This chapter delineates concrete guidelines, including the description of specific skills and therapeutic techniques. Each is specifically adapted for use with persons who define themselves as victims of childhood sexual abuse. These guidelines are also relevant for work with people who are wondering whether they might have been victims of abuse.

Two goals are of paramount and of equal importance:

1. These guidelines have been designed *to encourage the initial re-collection and/or disclosure of stories that may not have always been a part of clients' consciousness.*
2. These guidelines have been designed *to avoid therapist actions which may result in traumatic stories that later become viewed by the client as distorted.*

At the same time, however, this safe therapeutic environment will be carefully constructed to allow the client to tell his or her life story. In other words, we will be concerned with creating a therapeutic milieu that includes the components necessary for a disclosure to occur without undue influence from the professional.

These techniques prepare the therapist for the possibility of new and changing memories without an unnecessary focus on rehashing painful re-collections in search of the "true" story.

These goals are achieved by a focus through which the initial disclosure of the childhood abuse story is given particular, unique attention. The techniques suggested focus on encouraging the sharing of an abuse story with as little therapist influence as possible. Unlike narrative therapy practiced exclusively with persons who are sure of complete memories of trauma, these techniques prepare the therapist for the possibility of new and changing memories without an unnecessary focus on rehashing the painful re-collections in search of the "true" story.

The client is consequently freed from the burden of attempting to prove that his or her re-collections are historically accurate. In this way, the client is able to eventually focus on integrating re-collections of sexual abuse into a life story. Ultimately, that life story will feature the client as a strong, emotionally healthy person.

This chapter will cover techniques for creating the safe environment before, during, and after an initial disclosure takes place. If a client has an abuse story to tell, the helping environment will support the telling. If there is no abuse story to tell, the client will in no way feel compelled to develop one to meet the needs of the therapist.

At last, the therapist may relax and be ready to hear the words, "I never told anyone this before . . ."

In this way, the therapist need not fear that the helping process is somehow insisting that the client discuss abuse. Re-collections of childhood sexual abuse that might some day be retracted by the client are not likely to be discussed in this therapeutic milieu. On the other hand, the therapist need not fear that his or her concerns about "false" memories might not allow the client to discuss painful re-collections of childhood. At last, the therapist may relax and be ready to hear the words, "I never told anyone this before . . . "

SETTING THE STAGE

The drama of therapy occurs in a real time and place. The players improvise simultaneously. Light, sound, audience—all influence the unfolding situation. Any aspect of the helping environment that can be controlled by the therapist is available to use in the interest of facilitating the helping process.

If you can control it, you can use it to your client's benefit.

In other words, if you can control it, you can use it to your client's benefit. This means the therapeutic environment in its entirety—including time, place, and person—must be considered toward providing a perception of physical and emotional safety. This section will discuss such elements of the therapy environment as physical setting, confidentiality concerns, therapeutic boundaries, client choice, and the importance of relationship. Keep in mind that the goal is to create an atmosphere of safety before, during, and after a potential disclosure of childhood sexual abuse.

**Elements of the Therapeutic Environment
Available to Facilitate a "Safe Place":**

- *Physical setting*
- *Confidentiality*
- *Therapeutic boundaries*
- *Client choice*
- *Client-therapist relationship*

The Physical Setting

The most obvious, and perhaps most overlooked, aspect of the therapeutic environment is the physical setting. Therapy can occur almost anywhere: on the telephone, in client homes, in therapists' offices, at fast-food restaurants. A safe therapeutic environment, however, occurs in a safe physical place.

Safety and Trust: The Professional Use of Place

Persons who disclose painful re-collections almost universally speak of their ongoing search for safe places, safe relationships. Keep in mind that the group members described in previous chapters had trouble even conceiving of safety as either purely emotional or purely environmental. For them, physical and emotional safety were virtually inseparable, and exceedingly rare.

The client who is disclosing a traumatic story for the first time has never perceived a safe relationship in a safe environment. It is in the context of therapy that this safety is being experienced. This chapter includes general and practical guidelines and suggestions. Therapeutic techniques are described in detail for use with a broad-based consumer population. Special considerations for specific populations will be presented in the following chapters.

Creating a Safe Place

The therapist can consciously contrive to create a safe environment in a number of ways. A few are simple and concrete. Others are more subtle and refer to the tiny nonverbal components of communication that are so often unconscious. But what is therapy about if not making the unconscious conscious? The therapist must begin the process with a careful look at his or her own conscious and unconscious communications.

A Safe Place Is Private

As an example of an environmental influence with both concrete and abstract aspects, consider the issue of confidentiality. On the face of it, most experienced therapists are not uncomfortable with this concept. Informed consent is sought in the routine exchange of information. Policies are explained regarding the lack of confidentiality in situations of child or elder abuse and the clear and present danger of suicide or homicide. It is obvious to most clinicians that these policies must be clearly understood and explained to all clients in the first session, if not earlier. Many times clinicians follow the excellent practice of presenting these confidentiality policies in writing at the time of the initial appointment.

Yet it is easy to overlook more subtle flaws in the way we carry out this notion of protecting the privacy of clients. Not many therapists discuss with their clients how they will respond if they run into each other in the grocery store. Many times clients and therapists reside in the same general location. Many times people in service occupations, such as hairdressers, waiters, auto mechanics, and clergy, are aware of the therapist's line of work. To acknowledge an acquaintance with a person, then, is to open the door for the speculation that he or she is "one of those crazy people" with whom the therapist works. Small towns and rural areas are notorious for this kind of problem, but the same atmosphere can be created in an urban neighborhood or an affluent housing development.

It is incumbent on the therapist to consider the concerns that might weigh on a client's mind and pollute the safety of the therapeutic environment. Does the client share interests with the therapist—might they belong to the same health club? Perhaps they use the same post office, or their children attend the same ballet academy. The possibilities are endless, so the therapist must open them for consideration and discussion. It is usually safe to make a blanket statement on the order of, "If I happen to see you anywhere, I won't acknowledge that I know you unless you do so first." This gives the client the freedom to choose safe times and places to acknowledge his or her relationship with the therapist.

It is usually safe to make a blanket statement on the order of, "If I happen to see you anywhere, I won't acknowledge that I know you unless you do so first."

No Place Is Perfect

Some setting-related confidentiality concerns are even more subtle. In a solo practice, a therapist can schedule appointments with enough break time to facilitate a private entrance and exit from the office. But the waiting room of a group practice environment can be a violation of privacy for clients. For what reason would a person be sitting there, after all? We come to accept these things as normal, everyday occurrences, but considerations such as these can keep an abuse survivor with a story to tell from even getting to the therapist. The answer to this concern is to discuss the specific office setting in the initial phone contact. Home visits might be offered as an alternative for the first session. Or meetings can be scheduled at times when there is likely to be less chance of observation. The solution is not important. What is important is the therapist's willingness to empathize with a person who has hidden a painful story out of very real fears of retribution.

In the same way, the concrete shortcomings of a physical setting can be resolved in a variety of ways, provided they are open to discussion. Many therapists are sensitive to the fact that their offices are a reflection of who they are professionally. This makes it difficult for them to put location-related issues on the discussion table. For example, perhaps the accessibility and low rent of an inner-city office does not quite compensate for a less-than-desirable neighborhood. Or perhaps the prestigious, new office building across from a major medical facility has walls that are so thin that they allow voices to carry across individual therapists' offices. Maybe this prestigious building also houses a partial hospitalization program, potentially stigmatizing other consumers who enter at that door. These potential confidentiality concerns undermine the safety of the environment. A helping professional cannot afford to allow his or her private insecurities about office space to be an obstacle to client comfort.

Therapeutic Boundaries

A safe place requires predictability. Part of predictability in therapy is boundaries. The consideration of boundaries in the facilitation of the safe therapy environment is essential. This term is bandied about among therapists, but it is usually in the context of our concern for ourselves, as in "this client has no boundaries, she feels she can cancel at the last minute and call me at all hours the next week!" For the survivor of sexual abuse, however, this issue requires much more careful consideration.

Boundary violation: *an action outside of the expected role-related behaviors.*

What Are Boundaries, Anyway?

Keep in mind that sexual abuse is not defined in the same way by any two people. Most often, it is the violation of a boundary, *the action outside of the expected role-related behaviors*, that has caused the feelings of betrayal and the perceived violation of trust. Therefore, boundaries and boundary violations are among the most central issues for the work that lies ahead. They must be carefully outlined and frequently revisited to create a truly safe environment for the disclosure of traumatic life stories.

Therapeutic Management of Boundary Issues:

1. *Clearly outline—preferably in writing—how much notice is expected when a client cancels a session. Also clarify if and when such cancellations will result in a fee.*
2. *Clearly outline—preferably in writing—how much notice you will give should you need to cancel a session.*
3. *Describe specific situations which constitute "emergencies" that warrant after-hours calls.*
4. *Clearly outline the time frame within which you can be expected to respond to after-hours calls.*
5. *"Fess up" to your own boundary violations. Why have you consistently been running late? Why have you been spending an inordinate amount of time poring over your notes during sessions in which parent-child conflicts are being discussed?*

For example, certainly outline clearly when cancellations are expected and what constitutes an "emergency" that warrants an after-hours call. However, it is not advisable to gloss over your own late session start with a brief "I'm sorry" or hide a phone call answered during a session with a quick "Excuse me, please . . . you don't mind, do you?"

The person who has experienced many boundary violations is not equipped to manage such therapist-imposed violations. The client very often either does not mind (being used to such intrusions) or has no idea how to say he or she does mind (having had no practice in setting boundaries) or fully expects that the feeling (not just the expression, but the feeling itself) of being imposed upon will result in abandonment. How could this person possibly say, "Why, yes, I do mind that you are using my session time inappropriately?"

The establishment of healthy boundaries is the therapist's responsibility if a safe helping environment is to be created. Negotiate the rules of the therapeutic interaction carefully; for example, state that two missed appointments results in a fee. Once the rules are made, they will inevitably be broken. Discuss each instance and acknowledge your responsibility. If you have been running late for more than two sessions, acknowledge that to your client and be honest about it. Maybe you have been worried about money and have been overbooking yourself. Admitting to your own humanity can only make the client more comfortable with his or her own imperfections.

More difficult still than this little kind of confession is when your own personal issues are getting in the way of the client's comfort. Perhaps you have noticed that every time your client discusses his or her conflict with a parent you seem to take copious notes. You are not paying as much attention to your client as he or she deserves, and it is possible that the situation is due to your own conflict with a parent. Your client's therapy session is not the time or the place to discuss your problems with your mother, but it is possible to state that you might have a personal issue here. Apologize for your inattentiveness—again, acknowledging your very human vulnerabilities—and move on.

An example of the successful management of a boundary violation occurred in a session with a male, thirty-seven-year-old recovering alcoholic. He had told the therapist (female, twenty-seven) that he was not as committed to sobriety as he had once been. He refused to agree to total abstinence from alcohol. Consequently, she negotiated with him that she would not see him if he drank on the day of a scheduled session. She explained that this would be considered a last-minute cancellation and would therefore be billed to his account. Predictably, the client freely admitted having a drink before his session on the following week. When the therapist stated her intention of sticking by the agreement, the client was genuinely astonished. As she escorted him to the door, he exclaimed his disbelief that she would "throw him out" when he needed help. The therapist's response: "How could I ask you to trust me if I didn't do what I said I'd do?" This ended any further debate and freed the client from the anxiety of not knowing which behaviors were unacceptable.

> *Touch is an extraordinarily complex issue for the bearers of child-hood sexual abuse re-collections.*

Touch

A second, very critical boundary issue is that of physical touch. The planned use of touch can be a significant component in the therapeutic environment. However, touch is an extraordinarily complex issue for the bearers of childhood sexual abuse re-collections. The professional use of touch requires careful consideration in the creation of a safe environment for these clients.

Many persons who perceive an experience of severe physical and emotional violation based upon the unwanted touch of another have difficulties establishing their own boundaries about touch. Many of these people take pains to avoid any touch at all. Others are inappropriately free in soliciting and offering touch.

All clients experience the very human need for caring, affectionate touching. Studies related to the failure to thrive syndrome in human infants support this concept. Safe, predictable human touch is most probably part of any healthy, fulfilling human life. This component of comfortable touching is likely to be almost completely lacking for the survivor of childhood sexual abuse. Although the therapist can unfortunately resolve only the most minute part of that particular need, he or she can begin to provide a rudimentary, positive touching experience.

> *The therapist can begin to provide a rudimentary, positive touching experience—provided that touch is negotiated and renegotiated throughout the therapeutic experience.*

Many clinicians avoid touching clients entirely, due to the sexual connotation that could be superimposed onto the situation by a needy client. Others habitually hug clients or touch their forearms in a reassuring gesture. To the abuse survivor, each of these extremes has its dangers and is fraught with anxiety.

It is important that the therapist be aware of his or her issues regarding touch. These issues must be discussed with the client. The issue of touch is central to both the trauma and the recovery of the bearer of re-collections of childhood sexual abuse. This discussion of touch boundaries must be revisited again and again as therapy progresses.

For example, many therapists resolve the issue of touch boundaries with a pat request for permission ("Can I give you a hug?") that is used in all "touchable" situations. This solution is a bit too good to be true. The simplicity of the solution lies in its generalizability. Each person's touch issues are unique. They need to be brought to the therapy table, including the therapist's own. In short, touch must be carefully negotiated and renegotiated in the therapy session. An example of touch negotiations follows.

A female therapist (age thirty-three, Caucasian) working with a female client (age nineteen, Caucasian) created a safe enough environment for the client to disclose an instance of abuse that had not formerly been discussed. The client's life story included a well-documented experience of incest, from the ages of approximately four through sixteen, at the hands of a male cousin. The therapist and the client had been working together for approximately three months when the client disclosed a story of abuse with a female perpetrator. In many ways, this instance of abuse was more troubling to the client than those incidents that were well documented. She had strong feelings of revulsion as well as extreme shame and the fear that she might be homosexual as a result of the experience.

There is a great deal of grist for the therapeutic mill here. This first-time telling was clearly an important step in the therapy process. The rest of the example is related to touch specifically.

The therapist's comfort level with her own touch-related issues allowed the therapeutic progress to grow . . .

The therapist explained that due to her own culture, family of origin, and abuse history, she had a hard time initiating touch in most social instances. She openly and honestly disclosed that she was attempting to improve on her ability to offer touch to clients in an appropriate, therapeutic way. Then she stated that she would like to offer the client a hug, if the client would be comfortable in receiving it. "Just stay sitting if you're not comfortable and I won't get up either," the therapist suggested. Immediately, the client rose from her seat, giving the therapist the opportunity to get up also and comfort her with a brief hug. Afterward, the client was able to ask the therapist for a hug on several emotional occasions. The therapist's comfort level with her own touch issues allowed the helping progress to continue to grow. Ultimately, the client was able to experience personal control over when and how she was touched— perhaps for the first time in her life. An extension of this type of personal choice experience is elaborated in the following section.

Using Touch Therapeutically:

- *Be familiar with your own touch-related issues and be able to discuss them*
- *Be sure the client has complete control over when and how he or she is touched*

MAKING CHOICES, TAKING RESPONSIBILITY

A person who comes to believe he or she has been the victim of sexual abuse is not used to making even the most fundamental of choices. If sexual abuse is understood to be a crossing of expected boundaries and a manipulation and misuse of trust, it is clear that part of this person's life story is a chapter on feelings of extreme powerlessness. Thus, making choices and taking responsibility becomes part of the successful therapeutic environment. Client decision making needs to be predictable and expected. Occasionally, it will need to be demanded. It will not necessarily be comfortable for the client to meet the therapist's expectations of decision making, but these expectations can be introduced gently. If the expectations are consistent, the experience will become positive.

Client decision making needs to be predictable and expected—occa-sionally, it will need to be demanded.

Client choice must be an integral part of the therapeutic environment when stories of childhood trauma may be involved. If a client is unprepared to choose how and when to share a re-collection of childhood sexual abuse, he or she is vulnerable to sharing that re-collection as a way of meeting the perceived expectations of the therapist. In other words, the client is vulnerable to creating a life story that belongs to the therapist instead of the client. Consequently, the story might eventually be rejected entirely by the client. In addition to being antithetical to the treatment process, these situations are the very scenarios that create distorted perceptions of client life histories and therapist liability.

Without real choice, the client is vulnerable to creating a life story that meets perceived expectations of the therapist. This life story then belongs to the therapist, not the client. It may be a distortion that places the therapist in an ethically compromised and a legally vulnerable position.

Tiny Choices, Giant Consequences

For the bearer of re-collections of sexual abuse, making choices and taking responsibility for them is likely to be a long-forgotten process. When self-image includes the role of victim, the survivor needs to relearn choice-making skills. He or she is most probably used to allowing others to make all kinds of decisions.

The kind of passivity many victims manifest can affect decisions on many different levels. For example, a victim is likely to agree to an inconvenient or even impossible meeting time, while assuming that the professional who is arranging the meeting cannot or will not alter his or her schedule. A general feeling of powerlessness prevails for the re-collection bearer. It is this feeling of powerlessness that the therapist must challenge at every experiential opportunity.

For the client, the perception of powerlessness leads to a habitual avoidance of meeting personal needs. Since the client assumes that his or her needs will not be met, those needs tend to be ignored to the point of unconsciousness. In one instance, an adult victim of childhood sexual abuse was helping her parents with yard work. The project was extensive, involving a great deal of physical labor. The parents took frequent breaks to take a drink, sit down, or smoke a cigarette, but the memory bearer did not. She was hardly conscious that she was becoming tired and weak until the wheelbarrow she was pushing toppled over and carried her with it down a steep incline. Her leg was seriously injured.

Since personal needs are likely to be ignored by these clients, it is essential that the therapist give them as many choices as possible. It is also essential that the client be encouraged to make decisions when choices are available. For example, even the question, "Is two o'clock next Wednesday okay, or would you prefer three o'clock?", is often met with a blank stare from a client who has a history of victimization. The client then typically mutters some version of "It's up to you." Here the therapist must insist, sometimes repeatedly, that the client make the decision. If necessary, the question must be reframed and restated repeatedly. One client had cards with "yes" and "no" written on them. For weeks at the beginning of the helping process, she required yes-no questions that could be answered by showing one of the flash cards. Many times she held up both cards at once as a sign of her indecision. Once, she even tried to avoid a choice by crumpling the cards and eating them! Eventually, the flash cards became a pleasant jest and soon enough they were no longer necessary.

Ways to Facilitate Client Choice:

1. *Offer alternatives—in scheduling appointments, for example— and gently insist that the client make the choice.*
2. *Have the client choose when an incident will be discussed—this week or next, at the beginning of the session or the end.*
3. *Offer a client the opportunity to choose how a story is told—verbally, via journal entry, through a letter mailed to the therapist, etc.*

Decision making at this type of fundamental level is a prerequisite for a client to disclose a traumatic re-collection in a therapeutic manner. The client must be prepared to discuss the incident when he or she feels the time is right. After choosing the timing, it is best if the client can also choose the manner in which the re-collection is disclosed. Quickly blurted out at the close of a session or revealed in minute detail in a journal entry—the decision must be the client's. Otherwise, the therapist is at risk of imposing his or her values onto the therapeutic process and the client's re-collection itself.

Humor

In the previous example, decision making with yes-no flash cards became a pleasant jest. The jest itself is an important aspect of the therapeutic milieu. First of all, telling stories about the betrayal of trust that has characterized one's childhood is an extraordinarily painful topic that requires comic relief. If it is done carefully, humor can desensitize the most difficult of traumatic re-collections.

After many serious discussions about sexuality in the therapeutic setting, one adolescent girl was able to discuss an abuse experience with a fellow victim. The girls were cousins who had been simultaneously abused years before by an adult female. The vehicle that allowed them to discuss the experience that had gone unmentioned for nearly a decade was an illustrated book about masturbation. Their conversation began as a joke: "Look at this, we never tried that one!" The girls broke into gales of tension-releasing laughter. And in that split second of irreverence, the all-important initial disclosure was accomplished.

Many survivors of childhood sexual abuse have found the relationship *with a therapist to be what they needed to finally disclose their abuse re-collections.*

Relationship

It has frequently been suggested that the relationship between client and therapist is the catalyst that determines the success of the therapeutic endeavor. Many survivors of childhood sexual abuse have found the relationship with a therapist to be what they needed to finally disclose their abuse re-collections. Many survivors report

that their feelings of trust within the context of the helping relationship allowed them to take that leap of faith. They consistently report
that it was that first disclosure which was most instrumental in their
recovery.

Over and over again, I have been told by survivors that they
"trusted" their therapists. For these clients, however, this feeling of
trust in the therapeutic relationship is a bit like quicksilver. When
asked to pin it down, it seems to escape them. They search and
search for relationships in their lives in which they can trust; they
find the relationship with a therapist at last, and on that foundation
their process from victim to survivor begins. But when asked *why*
they trusted this particular therapist, *what* it was that made them feel
comfortable, *how* the relationship developed, they are simply bewil-
dered. The survivors, even those who have worked unsuccessfully
with countless therapists, do not seem to be able to identify what it
is that makes a helping relationship work.

Unfortunately, we therapists have not been any more successful.
The relationship between helper and client is widely acknowledged
to be a crucial aspect of successful therapy, but the variables that
allow it to happen are difficult to measure. It is the aspect of therapy
that therapists are likely to label "art, not science" and leave it at
that. Clearly, more research is needed in the area of the therapeutic
relationship.

SUMMARY: THE COMPONENTS
OF SUCCESSFUL THERAPY

It is proposed here that the therapeutic perspectives outlined in
the previous chapter provide the foundation for the successful, "art-
ful" creation of the helping relationship. To create a therapeutic
relationship with a person who may bear re-collections of childhood sexual abuse, three basic perspectives are necessary.

First, the memory of the traumatic event must be seen as a flexible narrative. This narrative need not be objectively proven to
anyone. The therapist is free to validate the emotions involved in
the telling without investigating the story's historical accuracy. In
addition, the client is free to highlight different aspects of the re-

collection as he or she progresses on the path from a self-identification of victim to a self-identification of survivor.

Therapeutic Behaviors That Facilitate the Development of Relationship

1. *Be willing to conduct nonaction as a therapeutic intervention.*
2. *Refrain from evaluating re-collections of trauma regarding their historical accuracy.*
3. *Be willing to allow the client to control the process of therapy when an important disclosure is imminent.*
4. *Maintain consistent boundaries. Be willing to candidly discuss boundary violations by therapist as well as client.*
5. *Negotiate and renegotiate confidentiality.*
6. *Facilitate client choice.*
7. *Maintain a safe physical setting.*

The second important perspective is that of recognizing the importance of a therapist's nonaction. A helping professional who realizes that stillness and silence facilitate the disclosure process is one who is ultimately successful in creating a safe therapeutic environment. In this environment, clients feel safe enough to tell their traumatic re-collections for the first time.

Finally, a therapist who is capable of building therapeutic relationships with bearers of traumatic re-collections is one who recognizes the importance of social process. This therapist will allow a client the power to occasionally control the social process involved in therapy. This helping professional is not likely to label breaches in decorum such as "door-knob comments" or "inappropriate" interruptions as evidence of pathology. Again, this perspective helps provide the foundation for the kind of helping relationship necessary to facilitate the first-time telling of traumatic life stories.

In addition to the foundation built on these three perspectives, the therapeutic techniques discussed in this chapter complete the necessary structure for the creation of an environment conducive to disclosures of traumatic memories. The elements of consistent boundaries, confidentiality, client choices, and safe physical setting complete that trusting relationship between clinician and client. Once created, the trusting relationship must be carefully maintained. Each element must be revisited and renegotiated as the helping process progresses. Ultimately, that trusting relationship facilitates the first-time disclosures of childhood sexual abuse.

Most significant, however, that relationship facilitates the disclosure in a therapeutically sound manner. The disclosure is not based on the needs or expectations of the therapist, nor does it reflect the therapist's values. Instead, the disclosure is part of a life narrative that is the client's own creation. Ultimately that therapeutically sound disclosure will lead the client through the self-identification process from victim to survivor.

Chapter 8

Special Considerations
for Special Populations

In this chapter, the special needs of special populations will be considered. The general perspectives and the specific techniques outlined in the rest of this book are generalizable to most work with adults who bear re-collections of childhood sexual abuse. However, particular consideration for work with members of special population groups is warranted.

The term "special populations" is the currently preferred means of referring to groups that face particular needs. These groups have formerly been referred to as "minorities," "disadvantaged groups," and "challenged" individuals. However, these terms have been discarded in light of the perception that they imply either a shortcoming or pathology in the group members or that they make light of the serious problems facing the groups.

Special populations are groups for whom the social environment is not sufficiently responsive.

Generally speaking, these are groups for whom the social environment is not sufficiently responsive. For example, it is now widely recognized that a person with a physical disability is not lacking in mobility; a conventional curb is lacking in accessibility.

This chapter begins with a discussion of general guidelines for work with special populations. This discussion includes consideration of the use of the ecosystem model (Morales and Sheafor, 1998) for assessing the unique needs of special populations, the use of the concept of eth-class (Devore and Schlesinger, 1991) in conducting ethnic-sensitive practice, and a general discussion of eliminating a fear of stereotyping as a means to increasing sensitivity to members of special population groups.

The chapter concludes with a discussion of situations specific to those special population groups likely to be encountered in work with adults who bear memories of childhood sexual abuse. The groups to be discussed include persons of racial diversity, persons with homosexual or bisexual orientation, persons who live in rural settings, men who carry re-collections of childhood sexual abuse, and older persons.

GENERAL GUIDELINES FOR WORK WITH SPECIAL POPULATIONS

Naming the Group

In today's "politically correct" climate, simply finding the appropriate name for a special population group is a challenge. For example, some persons of color prefer to call their ethnic affiliation "black," while others insist upon "African American," while still others disdain both designations. In all the confusion, a real danger is that the mainstream culture will return to the days of seeking to be "color blind" in terms of all types of diversity. The problem with the color blind perspective is that the very real needs of special population groups may easily be overlooked if everyone is considered equal. The social reality is that members of some groups face serious problems due to the inequities inherent in our social environment. If we hesitate to characterize those groups, we might easily avoid recognizing their problems and their needs. Therefore, characterize we must.

When the name of a particular group is in question, it quickly becomes apparent that all members of the group are not necessarily in agreement upon the appropriate title. For example, some indigenous American groups prefer to be known as Native Americans, some are not offended when called American Indians, and some prefer the precise name of their tribal affiliation. Still other situations are problematic when the mainstream society lumps several groups together—Asian Americans, for example. By so doing, the identity of a number of groups (Vietnamese, Korean, Indonesian) is blurred.

Determining the preferred title for a special population is easy; simply ask the client.

Fortunately, the practical solution to this very complex problem is simple. When working with a client, simply ask by what name that person prefers to identify his or her ethnic group. Ethnicity, by the way, is a cultural affiliation that serves as a way for persons to self-identify with a particular group. This is a different concept from that of race, which implies a purely genetic distinction. Occasionally, race and ethnicity overlap (as is the case for many Jewish people), but race and ethnicity may be very different (such as a biracial, black/Latina person who identifies with only an African-American ethnic group). In sum, distinguishing which special population group a client might embrace is important in that challenges unique to that group can be identified once the affiliation is known.

Eth-Class

In determining with which ethnic group a person identifies, it is important not to miss the concept of socioeconomic class. For example, sociologists have suggested that upper-class African Americans share more behavioral characteristics with upper-class Caucasian Americans than they do with working-poor African Americans.

"Eth-class" refers to the intersection of ethnicity and socioeconomic class.

The eth-class concept provides a means of understanding this situation in practice. Eth-class refers to the intersection of ethnicity and socioeconomic class. It explains "the role that social class plays in determining the basic conditions of life, while accounting for differences between groups at the same social class level" (Devore and Schlesinger, 1991, p. 20).

This concept helps clinicians to recognize that ethnicity shapes differences across all socioeconomic levels while not letting economic realities slip out of awareness when assessment is being made. When asking the question, "What do I need to know about my client?", the practitioner must develop an answer based on race, ethnicity, family, community, socioeconomics, and presenting problem.

The Ecosystem Model

The ecosystem model (Morales and Sheafor, 1998) is a means of managing this confusing array of a single client's group memberships. It is a model for implementing a holistic perspective in client assessment and thus efficiently recognizing the unique challenges faced by the client as a member of a number of groups.

Five Levels of Assessment for Special Populations:

1. Historical
2. Cultural
3. Community
4. Family
5. Individual

The model consists of five levels of identity: historical, cultural, community, family, and individual. Under the historical category, the clinician is reminded to consider the history of the client's ethnic group. Has there been a history of oppression for group members in this country? For example, this level of assessment makes the therapist cognizant of the fact that anyone of Japanese-American heritage shares a history of incarceration during World War II.

The cultural category asks the clinician to consider such factors as language: Is English a second language for this person? Will that result in potential miscommunication between client and therapist?

Next, community is considered: Is the community a strong support system for the client, or is it a source of stress? How strong is the individual's attachment to the community?

After considering the community, the family is evaluated in terms of its unique norms and values. The structure and behavioral expectations of each family are unique. The clinician conducting an assessment on the family level asks questions such as the following: Who makes the rules in the family? What are the roles occupied by each family member? Does the family supply emotional support to members? How? These unique qualities must be viewed in light of the expectations of the mainstream culture as well as those of the ethnic group.

At last, the individual is assessed as a unique person who lives in the intersection of this myriad of social forces. What are the biological, psychological, and social strengths and weaknesses? How can the individual's strengths be mobilized to compensate for environmental weaknesses?

In the following example, the ecosystem model and the eth-class concept will be utilized to assess the needs of several special population groups relative to the disclosure of re-collections of childhood sexual abuse.

SPECIFIC NEEDS OF SPECIAL POPULATION GROUPS

Persons Who Live in Rural Settings

The helping process is unique in rural settings, where nearly 25 percent of Americans reside. Generally speaking, human services are not as readily available as in urban areas. Persons are likely to rely upon family members for mutual aid and are therefore likely to bring a more serious presenting problem when they finally, in desperation, reach the therapy session. Keeping in mind the differences caused by economic realities, rural residents are likely to have a history of work either on farms or in industry close to home. As a result, they may be facing high levels of unemployment as corporate farming changes the economic face of their area. They are likely to be part of a culture that is homogeneous and consequently fears outsiders, persons of different ethnic groups, and sometimes helping professionals. The community itself may be close-knit and may be a potential resource for rural dwellers. Families are likely to be an important part of life, particularly extended families.

The clinician always checks his or her generalizations with the best available expert—the client.

Admittedly, these are all generalizations, educated guesses at best. These assumptions are not the same as stereotypes, however. Stereotypes are generally negative and are fixed ideas about the way other persons experience reality. Generalizations are made to identify the challenges particular to work with this special population, and they are not rigid ideas. The clinician always checks his or her generalizations with the best available expert—the client.

In sum, when working in a rural environment with persons who bear re-collections of sexual abuse, the clinician needs to be aware that the individual is likely to be facing serious difficulties that he or she is not able to manage using existing informal helping systems, such as the family and the church. He or she is likely to be wary of the professional and may therefore hesitate to reveal re-collections of trauma. This is particularly true if a family member is viewed as perpetrator, since loyalty to the family is likely to be deeply ingrained. Another factor that compounds the challenges of discussing abuse re-collections for persons in rural environments is the fact that people are often more aware of the actions of others in these small communities in which "everyone knows everyone else's business." This is not to say that clinicians ought to search for traumatic memories. Instead, they need to focus on developing the therapeutic relationship and frequently discussing confidentiality concerns. It is also helpful whenever possible to establish an inconspicuous office within the community served—even if it is a small, vacant room in a community church—rather than insisting that clients travel to the nearest metropolitan area to receive service.

Persons of Homosexual or Bisexual Orientation

Persons of homosexual or bisexual orientation face huge social challenges. Historically—and in the present—they have faced persecution. They are marginalized by the mainstream culture, to the point that couples are unable to legally marry (and share health insurance benefits) in most states. Unless they reside in an urban area with a large number of gay persons, they are likely to face community-based discrimination. In addition, community-based violence is an everyday reality to most members of this group.

Persons with a bisexual orientation face double jeopardy in the area of community approval: many persons with homosexual orientations shun bisexuals. They believe that bisexuality is merely a stepping stone for persons who are having difficulty managing their sexual orientation; therefore, they may view bisexuals as exacerbating the cultural problems faced by this special population group.

To complicate matters still further, many persons of bisexual or homosexual orientation are estranged from their families of origin. In short, the problems they face are innumerable.

Persons with homosexual or bisexual orientation may hesitate to share sexual abuse re-collections for fear that the trauma will be labeled as the "cause" of their sexual orientation.

On an individual level, many gay persons are currently wrestling with the commonly held belief that homosexuality or bisexuality is their "sexual preference." On the contrary, most believe that their sexual orientation has a genetic basis. For this reason, they will be hesitant to share sexual abuse re-collections for fear that the trauma will be labeled as the "cause" of their orientation. Likewise, many of these persons are very conscious that the helping professions formally labeled their sexual orientation as a pathology, and not so long ago. The clinician will have many obstacles in forming a therapeutic relationship with these persons, particularly if the clinician is heterosexual.

To provide quality service to this population, it is helpful to have the approval of an "insider." One major strength of this population is that a strong network of informal communication exists among group members. Clinicians can take advantage of this network by having a kind of word-of-mouth reference system that will help to assure persons of differing sexual orientations that this professional is sensitive to the needs of the group and open to learning about the group's concerns.

Persons of Racial Diversity

When the clinician is different from the client, the obstacles to the development of the therapeutic relationship are magnified. When working with persons whose race or ethnic group identification is different from the clinician's, the professional is best served by considering the eth-class concept and mentally working through the five steps of the ecosystem model. Ask your expert, the client, to delineate ways in which his or her situation is similar to or different from the educated generalizations produced by the assessment. Keep in mind that persons who are racially different from the white, mainstream society face discrimination and socioeconomic barriers in a society in which education is segregated by class and blacks are three times more likely to live in poverty than whites. Members of racial minorities may mistrust helping professionals and thus be less likely to disclose traumatic histories.

Keep in mind that persons who are racially different from the white, mainstream society face discrimination and socioeconomic barriers . . .

By the same token, if the clinician's racial, ethnic, and socioeconomic situation is very similar to the client's, relationship building will be facilitated. But the clinician may be blind to the impact of cultural, community, or family influences. Therefore, a consideration of the needs of the clinician's population is in order. A therapist who engages in a meaningful supervisory process will find this to be an excellent environment for exploring his or her own cultural biases.

Finally, when considering the issue of child sexual abuse, the clinician is well advised to keep in mind the relative definition of abuse. Different ethnic groups have differing expectations and norms regarding child rearing, and it is best for the professional to be informed about characteristics of the ethnic group with which the client identifies.

Seniors

Persons over the age of sixty-five are the fastest growing segment of the U.S. population. As more people get older, it is becoming recognized that psychotherapy can be very useful with this population. As time goes by, it will be more and more likely that any clinician will offer services to seniors.

In this society, economic challenges are very real for older persons. They face the detrimental effects of ageism in the work environment through forced retirement and prejudicial hiring practices. Many also face the challenges of living on a fixed income; despite the cost of living increase to Social Security benefits, approximately 12 percent of our older people live in poverty.

Older persons grew up in an era when discussions of sexual behavior and sexuality were even more taboo than they are today. This presents an obstacle to discussions of childhood abuse.

In addition, elder abuse is a reality. Seniors who live in households in which younger generations are faced with caregiving responsibilities, in which there is a history of substance abuse or mental illness, or in which the younger generation is dependent upon an older family member are at risk for sexual, physical, and financial abuse in the present.

Older persons grew up in an era when discussions of sexual behavior and sexuality were even more taboo than they are today.

Gender As a Special Population

Women are generally seen as the special needs group when it comes to discussion of gender. However, when considering recollections of childhood sexual abuse, the opposite is true. Men in our society are not enculturated to discuss emotional issues. Consequently, they are less likely than women to seek professional help for emotional problems; therefore, childhood sexual abuse may be even more detrimental for them than it is for women.

Men in our society are not enculturated to discuss emotional issues, they are less likely than women to seek professional help for emotional problems; therefore, childhood sexual abuse may be even more detrimental for them than it is for women.

For the clinician, this means that sensitivity to these issues is required. This society does not train men to freely express painful emotions, so re-collections of trauma are likely to be presented in a rational, intellectualized way. As has been noted, this is not necessarily an obstacle to the therapeutic process. Discussions of traumatic events need not always be accompanied by emotional expression to be processed in a healing fashion.

CONCLUSION

Work with adult bearers of re-collections of childhood sexual abuse requires a firm foundation in a professional, helping relationship. The process of building such a relationship is complicated when clients are members of special population groups. The clinician is well-served by considering the problems faced by special populations—areas in which the social environment is not sufficiently responsive—prior to the first session. In this way, the relationship-building process will be facilitated and an environment will be created in which traumatic re-collections can be discussed in a therapeutic fashion.

Chapter 9

Troubleshooting

In this final chapter, unique techniques and troubleshooting guidelines will be presented for work with specific situations. Although the perspectives and techniques previously outlined are generalizable to most work with bearers of childhood sexual abuse re-collections, a few caveats are in order for some situations.

Some situations present particular challenges.

Throughout this book, it has been made clear that there are several basic goals in working with persons who may bear re-collections of childhood sexual abuse. First, the therapist must create an environment conducive to sharing the traumatic stories. As the stories are disclosed for the first time, the therapist must exercise special caution not to influence the stories with his or her own values and priorities. Methods for meeting these therapeutic goals have been outlined, but some situations present particular challenges.

This chapter comprises three sections of common challenges. The first section deals with particular client groups that require special consideration, including persons who are wondering whether their experiences constitute abuse, clients who have been told by other therapists that they "must have" experienced abuse, work with nonverbal persons, and other specific populations.

The second section deals with the important aspect of family in work with persons who bear re-collections of childhood sexual abuse. This controversial area of work will be addressed in light of the life narrative perspective of traumatic incidents.

Finally, the chapter concludes with a section related to work as a member of a professional treatment team. Most practitioners are part of a formal or informal group of professionals, including psychiatrists, case workers, therapists, and others, who all have contact with any individual client. Cooperation among the members of this team of professionals is quite obviously in the client's best interest, but presents special challenges often overlooked in discussions of appropriate treatment. Again, the goal is a therapeutic atmosphere that facilitates disclosure of traumatic re-collections without the undue influence of any professionals.

UNIQUE CLIENT POPULATIONS

Therapy Veterans

Many clients have had the experience of being in therapy for a variety of reasons with persons who do not share similar therapeutic perspectives. In some infamous cases, clients have reportedly been told that they have "symptoms" of a history of sexual abuse and that they must strive to remember this history. Some of these men and women have come to believe that they have been abused; others seek another professional opinion. These persons enter therapy for the second time with the explicit goal of determining whether they have histories of abuse.

These persons enter therapy for the second time with the explicit goal of determining whether they have histories of abuse.

These situations are challenging for a number of reasons. First, it is almost never advisable to denigrate the work of colleagues. One of the reasons psychotherapy works is because people have at least some faith that it does. In addition, a client's report of past treatment is by its very nature secondhand. It is imperative in these situations to get a release signed and speak to the previous therapist or, at the very least, have written records of past treatment forwarded. Perhaps the comments of other professionals have been misconstrued by the client. If a client should refuse to give consent to this type of information gathering, it may be symptomatic of more serious problems. The issue needs to be explored fully before any other work can be done.

It is imperative in these situations to get a release signed and to speak to the former therapist . . . at the very least, have treatment records forwarded.

Another serious challenge in these situations is the ever-present legal liability. Increasing numbers of clients are developing re-collections of abuse only to retract them at a later date. Rather than focusing on the presence or absence of traumatic re-collections, it is nearly always preferable to keep the work focused on current life situations. An understanding of the process of trauma resolution as outlined earlier in this work suggests that a troubling re-collection will repeatedly push its way into consciousness. When that happens as a natural consequence of life events or increasing levels of self-understanding, the initial disclosure will occur. There is no need to push that process. If the guidelines presented here are followed, the therapeutic environment will facilitate a disclosure when the time is right for the client.

A troubling re-collection will push its way into consciousness. When that happens as a natural consequence of life events or increasing levels of self-understanding, the disclosure will occur. There is no need to push that process.

If possible, it is usually preferable to allow the client to determine the speed at which therapy progresses. To purposefully search for traumatic memories is counterproductive to the process of empowering clients to be the authors of their own life stories. They are best left to tell their stories in their own way, in their own time. A safe therapeutic environment is likely to be a patient, accepting environment.

A safe therapeutic environment is likely to be a patient, accepting environment.

Clients Who Are Pressed for Time

On the other hand, we do not always have the luxury of allowing the therapeutic process to unfold in its own time. In many situations, time limits are imposed on the helping process. For example, some clients feel compelled to visit and revisit their traumatic recollections because they are concerned that some other person—usually a child—may currently be at risk. In these cases, it is best to err on the side of safety, of course, and protect anyone who may be vulnerable. However, this must be done with extreme caution where family members are concerned. Some of the complex issues related to potential estrangement from family members will be discussed later in this chapter.

Some clients feel compelled to visit and revisit their traumatic recollections because they fear some other person—usually a child— might currently be at risk.

As a stopgap measure, the client can be taught to become a confidant in a general way for the child who is feared to be at risk. The client can then share with the child basic self-protection measures, such as saying "no" to unwanted touch. This can be done without making the child distressed about impending danger and can serve the purpose of maintaining a healthy environment for the child as well as peace of mind for the client.

The client can share basic self-protection measures with the child.

In another time-related situation, occasional legal requirements will force a focus on the past that may be antithetical to recovery. For example, some cases involving litigation and repeated testimony continue to place a focus on producing an "accurate" story of events. In work with young children in particular, this is a difficult and unfortunate consequence of the legal system. Often the best a therapist can do in these situations is offer an environment in which the traumatic event does not have to be discussed. Nonverbal work can be extremely beneficial in these cases. (See, for example, Simonds, 1994.)

Some cases involving litigation and repeated testimony continue to place a focus on producing an "accurate" story of events.

Finally, the demands of the managed care environment or other funding availability may place time restrictions on the therapeutic environment. Here time-limited, goal-focused treatment is likely to be the order of the day. This is not necessarily antithetical to the process of allowing disclosures of traumatic life stories to unfold at the client's own pace, however. If therapist and client remain focused on present concerns, the disclosures that are relevant to the client's developing self-understanding and life narrative will come to the fore. Other re-collections may have to wait for some future intervention, but this is not likely to have deleterious results if the therapist does not place undue focus on the need to discuss re-collections quickly and in detail.

Often the best a therapist can do in these situations is to offer an environment in which the traumatic event does not have to be discussed.

In this type of situation, the most likely negative impact of time-limited treatment comes from the helping professional's own issues. If the therapist believes a managed care environment denigrates the value of his or her work, it is easy to project that discomfort onto the client. Suddenly, the "system," the insurance provider, the funding source, is seen as invalidating the client's need for ongoing therapy. In reality, the client is likely to be capable of using available therapy time in an efficient manner. His or her feelings of invalidation at time-limited treatment plans are likely to be exacerbated or even created by the therapist's feelings of professional invalidation. Clearly, the therapist must examine these issues in a competent supervisory setting.

The client's feelings of invalidation at time-limited treatment plans imposed by funding sources are likely to be exacerbated—or even created—by the therapist's own feelings of professional invalidation.

A Timing Mistake

The issue of time-limited treatment suggests another, related concern—demand for work. A therapist who is skilled at making a demand for work will give clients the opportunity to use therapy sessions efficiently. However, when the sharing of re-collections of sexual abuse are part of the therapy process, this skill is difficult to master. An apparently unsuccessful demand for work from my own practice follows.

In this situation, a high-functioning, Caucasian woman in her twenties had mentioned early in the course of treatment that she wondered if she had a history of abuse. This client developed a pattern of attending scheduled appointments only if in crisis and cancelling all other appointments, sometimes dropping out of sight for many months at a time. Sessions that she did attend took on an air of consultation—very present-focused and usually consisting of answers to a series of questions posed by the client (e.g., "People who grow up in substance-abusing families sometimes face this or that problem, right?").

After approximately six sessions of this nature, I sought to make a demand for work. I suggested that the client consider attending a session when a crisis was not occurring in order to explore more fundamental issues. The client was reminded that she had once suggested that she wondered whether she had a history of abuse, and this was used as an example of some of the issues that might be considered in work which was more of a preventative nature than her usual crisis-intervention requests.

Normally, this would be a useful way of making a demand for work. The client was being gently confronted with the fact that her intellectual approach to treatment was not addressing the issues underlying the everyday problems. Unfortunately, because this client's issues included the possibility of childhood sexual abuse, perhaps the demand for work was too threatening. When the therapist implied that such work would "take some time," it is possible that the client imagined weeks and weeks of sessions, since it is often assumed that long-term therapy is needed to recover from a history of abuse. The client cancelled the next session and did not reschedule, effectively ending therapy.

Instead of suggesting that such work "takes time," it is recommended that the therapist guide the client to the work one session at a time. It is not necessary to contract for extended treatment as long as the verbal contract for work includes the possibility that sessions might continue as needed. In this way, the client can be guided toward accomplishing the "real" work of therapy without being overwhelmed at the prospect of addressing abuse issues, and short-term treatment may be used (and reused at a later date) to the client's benefit.

Take whatever steps are possible to increase the client's ability to communicate.

Stories Without Words: Nonverbal Clients

Although short-term treatment is not necessarily problematic in therapy with bearers of childhood sexual abuse re-collections, some situations do require extra time. Cases that involve young children, adults with severe developmental disabilities, persons with speech pathologies or head injuries, and others who are simply less articulate than the average person present unique challenges in work with disclosures of traumatic re-collections. As in all situations, the goal of treatment is to facilitate an environment conducive to sharing the re-collection, but what is to be done when the ability to share information is drastically compromised? First, keep in mind that historically accurate reports of life events are not the focus of treatment. Next, take whatever steps are possible to increase the client's ability to communicate. For example, one client with severe mental retardation had great difficulty getting others to understand the most simple communications. He resided in a community living arrangement and attended a sheltered workshop for day programming. As a result, he continually experienced staff turnover and new persons who did not have enough history with him to understand most of his attempts at articulation.

For this young man, the focus of the helping process became the development of very concrete methods to facilitate communication. The consistency of the relationship with the therapist allowed the client to make himself understood, and a word processor facilitated the literal creation of a life story that could be printed out and shared weekly at his discretion. Eventually, therapy facilitated the development of a kind of newsletter of important weekly events that he could choose to share with significant others. At last, he was able to disclose traumatic childhood events in this context and was greatly empowered in his newfound ability to create a life story and share it with others at his own discretion.

Other nonverbal means of creating stories have also been successfully demonstrated. The use of metaphor in play therapy, for example, is well documented. In addition, the use of journals for the development of self-awareness is also widely used. One caveat related to journals: just as the perspective presented here does not focus on the telling and retelling of traumatic stories, it likewise does not support the use of journal keeping focused on seeking out traumatic re-collections. A daily journal focusing on the painful events of childhood is not conducive to integrating those re-collections into a healthy life narrative. On the other hand, the judicious use of a journal is a way of creating a safe environment for the disclosure of traumatic re-collections in that clients are supported in the nonverbal, pressure-free sharing of their stories. The journal can then be a resource during the therapy session. Some clients also prefer mailing their journals prior to therapy sessions as a less threatening manner of sharing their emerging life narratives. (See Simonds, 1994, and Dayton, 1990, for nonverbal techniques of exploring traumatic re-collections.)

These types of "once-removed" vehicles for disclosing difficult re-collections may also be useful with populations other than nonverbal clients. For example, men commonly face a much more difficult challenge in sharing abuse re-collections than women and can benefit from techniques that facilitate storytelling without words. Specific disclosures related to such topics as current sexual orientation concerns, performance issues, and difficulty making healthy sexual choices may be closely tied to a first-time disclosure of a sexual abuse re-collection. The difficulty of discussing such sensitive issues can be alleviated through these nonverbal techniques.

Taken together, these considerations point to the fact that each client has his or her own life story to develop and to tell. The special needs of particular client groups ought to be considered to facilitate the telling of that story, including any disclosures of abuse re-collections that might become significant relative to the developing life story and the client's developing self-image.

THE ROLE OF FAMILY

The development of a client's life story and self-image has undoubtedly been highly influenced by family experiences. Whether the family is defined by the client as a family of orientation, a family of procreation, or an alternative family form, this social unit is undeniably the most influential force in a client's life and life story.

Families function in numerous ways as societal institutions. They facilitate economic cooperation among members, they legitimize sexual relationships, and they provide socialization for children.

Families take innumerable forms in our complex society. The American family is as diverse as its multiple influences of race, ethnicity, religiosity, and socioeconomic class. Authority, be it patriarchal, matriarchal, or some other arrangement, differs by family type. The level of family autonomy within the larger society differs by family type and current social policy. The type of socialization provided to children—cultural values, roles, and self-concept—differs among family types and ethnic groups. Overall, our rapidly shifting social scene continues to produce new family patterns.

However, all of this family diversity exists in the context of the persistence of traditional family forms. Americans continue to value the family and recognize it as a refuge from the outside world.

The family is perhaps the last remaining social unit that is expected to provide its members with emotional security. Despite the changing forms of families, most of us still think of the family as the place "where when you have to go there, they have to take you in." With the possible exception of some closed religious communities, there is no other comparable social unit in our culture.

All of this is to say that the family is a unique and very precious commodity in this society. All too often, helping professionals get caught up in judging and condemning the families of the clients we serve. This is an understandable phenomenon. As we develop empathy for our clients and their perceptions of childhood trauma, it is easy to feel protective of them. Clients who disclose first-time stories of childhood sexual abuse are quite likely to be directly incriminating a family member as they share those re-collections. (How could he or she hurt our client that way?) If the blame is not direct, it is likely to be present in an indirect form. (Why didn't someone protect the client, why didn't they listen when he or she tried to tell?)

It is all too easy for professionals to place blame on families, to judge families, even to encourage estrangement from families.

First-time disclosures of childhood sexual abuse re-collections are often horrific stories. As a result, it is all too easy for professionals to place blame on families, to judge families, even to encourage estrangement from families. In response to this situation, consider this: a therapist who supports a client's estrangement from family members does so at that client's peril, since there is no guarantee that the client will be able to re-create a new family.

Validate feelings of betrayal, hurt, and anger. Support the new relationship boundaries that develop as clients come to understand their traumatic re-collections and the impact they have had on their lives. Work to facilitate clients' deepening understanding of their unique families, their strengths, and their weaknesses.

If at all possible, work to prevent any further trauma within the family. However, seek to accomplish that protection by promoting positive family interactions. Once again, a therapist who supports a client's complete alienation from family members does so at that client's emotional peril. Take away a client's family—dysfunctional as it may be—and with what, with whom, will you replace it?

In one difficult family situation, a survivor of sexual abuse participated in family therapy along with her parents. The client had a history of residential treatment throughout most of her adolescence. The parents were defensive initially; later, they said they had had many experiences in which professionals bluntly told them they were the cause of their child's problems. The therapist initially spoke only to the family as a unit, never to one individual when no one else was present. Within a few months, the parents as well as the young survivor developed a trusting relationship with the therapist. Ultimately, the extended family members who had been estranged were reunited. While some extended family members would never acknowledge that they "believed" the client's abuse story, they were able to begin the process of healing the family. In this situation, the process began in time for the client and a grandparent to make peace prior to the grandparent's death. Such family relationships are invaluable and occur only within the context of the family itself.

WORK IN THE CONTEXT OF THE TREATMENT TEAM

In some cases, particularly where a funding source mandates regular treatment team meetings including professionals and clients, some of the traditional roles of the family are fulfilled by the treatment team itself. The treatment team can become the source of socialization, self-concept, and values formulation for many children and adults who bear re-collections of childhood sexual abuse.

In these situations, the client may experience dysfunctional relationship patterns in the treatment team similar to those he or she experienced in the family. This occurs in situations in which clients are encouraged to actively participate in treatment planning; that is, any situation in which treatment is provided with funding mandates that include interagency treatment planning. In such cases, professionals may disagree on treatment goals and interventions, professional egos may be bruised, and power may be negotiated behind the scenes. Unhealthy alliances may be formed. Professionals sometimes step out of their roles, occasionally creating relationships with clients that resemble friendships. In these situations, a first-time disclosure of a traumatic re-collection is likely to be lost in its potential as a vehicle for client growth. More likely, the emerging life story is greeted with an implication of which professional is the client's "favorite!"

Team members should not fear mistakes, but should embrace them as learning experiences among equals.

It is imperative, then, that professionals facilitate cooperation among themselves as participants of a treatment team. Where funding mandates a meeting schedule, it is best to undertake the formality in a spirit of genuine collaboration. Where there is no formal treatment team, one professional must take the lead in facilitating regular, open communication among all persons involved. Just as one would hope to create cooperation and open dialog in a family, the treatment team can strive for these goals as well. Team members should not fear mistakes, but should embrace them as learning experiences among equals. And in the treatment team, of course, the client is the first among these equals. He or she is likely to rise to the challenge of being in charge of the treatment team and grow from the experience.

Finally, therapists would be well-served to remain cognizant of the fact that there is much to be learned about disclosures of re-collections of childhood sexual abuse. For that reason, professionals of various perspectives can learn from one another. In addition, we can all learn from our clients—if we are able to fully engage in listening. This attitude will facilitate the growth of knowledge as well as remind us that a first-time disclosure might be treated as any other opportunity for client growth. These emerging life narratives need not be stalked or feared. Instead, they can be accepted as they come—as they undoubtedly will—to the carefully prepared therapeutic environment.

EDITING THE TRAUMATIC STORY

This final section presents some general guidelines for proceeding with the therapeutic process once a re-collection of childhood sexual abuse has been disclosed. Once it has been told, the resulting emotions must be validated. Then comes the process of integration into the healthy life story, the process of narrative repair.

Once a traumatic re-collection has been disclosed, the resulting emotions must be validated . . . then the process of integration begins.

Narrative Repair

When life narratives as presented by clients do not seem credible, validation alone may not be an appropriate therapeutic response. It has been suggested that stories may "fail" as social communication for two reasons: first, they lack essential information, and second, they are unconvincing (Robinson and Hawpe, 1994, p. 121). It makes sense that stories cannot be effective organizers of perceptions if they are not credible in the cultural context in which they are related to self and others. Stories may lack credibility for a number of reasons, including the anxiety level of the teller. However, it is a difficult challenge for the clinician to validate a client's story while assisting, as story editor, to help make the client sound credible to his or her potential audience.

It has been suggested that the therapeutic process that flows from the narrative perspective includes a therapist who functions in the role of co-editor of the life story (Parry and Doan, 1994). This editing process results in an altered life story that functions to reconstruct identity (Sands, 1996). As co-editor, the therapist must balance twin goals of client autonomy and need for direction.

Some suggestions have been postulated for the resolution of stories generated in the therapeutic setting that seem to lack credibility. Where life stories lack credibility, therapist and client may engage in narrative repair. Methods of narrative repair have been described by a variety of therapists, who usually include analogy as a problem-solving device. (See, for example, Parry and Doan, 1994; Hunter, 1994; and McAdams, 1993.) In other cases, narratives may be more effectively presented to audiences as stories in search of explanations, thus effectively transferring the narrative task to the audience (Robinson and Hawpe, 1994).

Life narratives are not factual accounts of events.

Editing the Narrative

It has been suggested (Parry and Doan, 1994) that life narratives may be employed as the focus of the helping process. Initially, clients are challenged to tell stories drawn from the lives of others. This process is significant in that it enables clients to see that life narratives are not factual accounts of events:

> When the very notion that there is one true story is thrown into question, people begin to realize that any story is just a story. They are free to invent stories of their own that serve the purpose of any narrative: to provide a framework of meaning and direction so that a life may be lived intentionally. (pp. 5-6)

In so doing, the therapist functions as a kind of editor, as could other group members in a group therapy context.

Using narrative therapy with adult survivors of childhood sexual abuse clearly has a number of advantages: first, it empowers the client to write a personal life narrative of past, present, and future events; second, it provides a vehicle for the power of group interaction to be used in a focused and beneficial manner, avoiding the possible negative influences of group interaction.

Any editing of the story must be done with extreme caution, at the initiation of the client and with a focus on his or her own voice.

On the other hand, however, some cautions are in order. Since the very telling of the abuse story for the first time is so difficult for this population, and because validation of the emotions involved in the telling is so significant to the safe and trusting atmosphere necessary for the work to proceed, any editing of the story must be done with extreme caution. It would be prudent to do so only at the initiation of the client and with a focus on his or her own voice:

> . . . quite often the clients seeking our editorial services have *not* been the major authors of the stories they relate to us in therapy. Much of the time it seems that they have been more "readers" than "writers," and are blindly living out a mythology (a shared story) that they were handed very early in life. . . . In therapy, it is often necessary to begin the process of the client's becoming her/his own author. . . . (Parry and Doan, 1994, pp. 102-121)

Sharing the Story

The therapeutic process in which clients become conscious authors of their own life stories highlights an additional caution for work with this population. Family members appear to be extremely important to this group. An inability to share an abuse story with family members can be the source of significant distress, such as that exhibited by Catherine. On the other hand, ongoing invalidation of one's abuse story can also be extremely detrimental, as demonstrated by Charlene. Numerous persons who view themselves as survivors of childhood sexual abuse sever ties with families of origin, an action that is sometimes encouraged in the popular recovery movement.

The family can create a family story that does not invalidate the client's individual story.

Clearly this important issue must be carefully considered by therapists. The decision to share the abuse story with family members must be a process directed by the client in consultation with the therapist. Once this decision has been made, it is possible to co-edit the story toward credibility without risking that a narrator will perceive invalidation. That is, the family itself can create a family story that may be slightly different from—but not invalidating of—the client's individual story.

Clinicians may not be as skeptical of popular beliefs as they ought to be.

Finally, in response to the controversy surrounding adult re-collections of childhood sexual abuse, mental health practitioners need to respond through knowledge development. Clinicians should be careful consumers of research, using wisdom gained through practice anecdotes judiciously. Armed with knowledge, therapists may offer clients appropriate service. A concern high-lighted by this study is that clinicians may not be as skeptical of popular beliefs as professionals ought to be.

Another concern demonstrated by this study is that persons who are actively wondering if they have had childhood sexual abuse experiences may be underserved. By not offering services to these persons out of the fear of implanting false memories, we may be demanding that they become sure they are victims before they seek our help. By employing the perspectives and techniques offered here, the clinician can prepare the therapeutic environment and comfortably accept what life narratives emerge within it.

Appendix

Research Methods

The research that provided the data for this book took a myriad of forms. The issues of concern were broad, and a holistic approach was required. This appendix provides a general description of the research questions addressed, methods of data collection and analysis, methods of verification, and research limitations. In addition, some caveats regarding this type of research are presented.

RESEARCH QUESTIONS

A number of research questions are relevant to an objective look at adult re-collections of childhood sexual abuse. These are related to the group interaction and social conditions that provide the context for the development and disclosure of re-collections. In addition, they are related to the effect of such re-collections on the group members. In the clinical setting, it is the function of re-collections, rather than their historical accuracy, that is of interest. These questions are consequently not related to the historical accuracy of the re-collections; instead, they address their development and the interactional circumstances that facilitate their disclosure:

1. How does psychosocial trauma come to be conceptualized and disclosed as re-collections of childhood sexual abuse in the therapeutic setting?
2. What is the role of the therapist in the development of these re-collections?
3. What happens in a therapeutic setting when re-collections are revealed? Are there shifts in kinesics, voice pitch, rhythm of interaction?

METHOD

The research method applicable to this inquiry is ethnographic microanalysis. This approach to the study of human interaction has been derived from context analysis, the ethnography of communication, Goffman's perspective regarding the interactional presentation of self, conversation analysis, and interactionally focused forms of general ethnography (Erickson, 1992a). A small body of literature has been developed in which the therapeutic session has been treated as a communication event in an extensive manner (e.g., Borgotta, Fanshel, and Meyer, 1960; Fanshel and Moss, 1971; Labov and Fanshel, 1977; Scheflen, 1973). More recently, Ferrara (1994) has treated the therapy session as a specifically professional communication event through discourse analysis. This study builds on these largely structural analyses by providing an holistic, yet statistically verifiable, perspective.

PARTICIPANTS AND SETTING

A convenience sampling method was used. Much of the preliminary data came from my own clinical practice. Other data were the result of interviews with other practitioners, usually within the context of clinical supervision I provided. The bulk of the data presented, however, comes from a series of group therapy sessions. The specific setting chosen for this study was a therapeutic group facilitated by a master's-level social worker. This naturalistic group was geared toward women of working age who had troubling childhood memories that they believed might be related to histories of sexual abuse. The women were all service recipients through a county mental health/ mental retardation office and were identified as having chronic mental health needs. Each lived in a loosely structured, community residential setting in which supervision is provided on a part-time, as-needed basis. Payment for group participation came from group members and was supplemented by Medicare benefits. Each group member was originally referred by a mental health professional in addition to self-identifying as a sexual abuse survivor.

The sample was based on the willingness of the group facilitator and group members to participate. The group was conducted outside the auspices of an agency; therefore, informed consent was obtained from the therapist and group members for both participant observation and videotaping of group sessions and interviews. A privately run group was chosen under the assumption that a private group facilitator would be less likely to be anxious about being observed, since there is no concern about a supervisor judging the work unfavorably. In addition, the private therapist identified as a participant was genuinely motivated to learn about ways to improve her work.

Access

Access difficulties arose whenever the cooperation of private, nonprofit agencies was sought for research of this type. Upper-level supervisors consistently denied research access. Each time, the stated reason was the vulnerability of the population of abuse survivors, a group deemed too fragile to participate in a research endeavor. In one case, an agency had procured legal privilege for its therapists. The researcher could attend an agency-based training and also procure this relatively complete legal protection on behalf of research participants. Despite this relatively rare legal protection, access was still denied. The agency director feared that transcripts of group process could be subpoenaed and could potentially be harmful to the agency or clients despite confidentiality assurances.

Informed Consent

Informed consent regarding participation in the study was sought from group members just prior to the first session. This approach was taken due to the small number of group members. Each was interviewed by the researcher individually; anything but unanimous agreement would have interrupted the study. To deal fairly with participants concerning the sensitive issue of videotaping therapeutic group sessions, specific permission was sought from each individual for videotaping in addition to permission to be observed, interviewed, and audiotaped by the researcher. Along with the assurance that they would never be named, participants were given the power to have any segment of any tape (audio or video) erased up to forty-eight hours after it was taped. Part of the informed consent process in this case included assurance that the tapes would not be used for demonstration purposes. All transcription was done by the researcher. All tapes were ultimately erased.

DATA COLLECTION

Participant observation in conjunction with videotaping of the time-limited series of groups was the major method of data collection. Field notes were taken during sessions for the sake of accuracy as well as to give group participants the impression that the researcher was occupied with some task. Although the researcher was able to unobtrusively glance at the group participants, prolonged observation and eye contact was avoided to keep the researcher's impact on the group process to a minimum.

An examination of the social context was conducted prior to the participant observation of the group process over a two-and-one-half-year period. This examination included a review of scientific literature as well as television, popular magazines, and local newspapers; formal and informal social welfare policy; professional conference attendance; and informal interviews with key informants. Documents directly relevant to the group, such as participant handouts and participants' written task assignments, were also employed in the final analysis to triangulate conclusions.

Limitations

As with any study that is in any part ethnographic in nature, this study is limited to the extent that the entire context of any social event cannot be presented in any report. Just as the camera is focused on one area of the therapy room, the researcher too has a limited perspective. To respond to this inherent limitation, this report includes as much information as possible about the researcher, the research agenda, and the social context of the data-gathering process. In this way, it is hoped that the reader will have sufficient information to independently judge the validity of conclusions.

The data source is limited. Ethnographic studies are generally much longer than the data-collection phase of this short-term group, even when the follow-up interviews are considered. Findings, however, are likely to be transferable due to their applicability to practice with survivor groups in general, as demonstrated by the validity interviews. Also, findings may be transferable to the degree that they represent the interactional elements shared in common by all human communication.

In view of the controversy regarding recovered memories of childhood sexual abuse, this study does not include the full range of variation in the first-time narrative of such re-collections. While the discrepant case (i.e., the person who dropped out of group) provides an example of someone who did not share any abuse re-collections with the group, the first-time re-collections analyzed here were not experienced by the group members as recovered memories. That is, like other persons discussing old memories of childhood abuse for the first time (Gasker, 1993), these women perceived them to be about incidents they always knew had happened. They were not brand-new memories; they were first-time discussions of them. It is impossible to determine at this point whether all bearers of re-collections of childhood abuse have this same perception or whether some actually do perceive the memories to concern events they never knew had happened.

Finally, some (or perhaps most) findings are likely to be specific to this particular group. Some aspects of the environment and the individual participants are examples of a unique situation that will not be replicated. This, in and of itself, has some value for work with survivors of sexual abuse who suffer from mental illness, since it has been suggested recently that future research ought to explore possible differences between subpopulations of survivors (Donaldson and Cordes-Green, 1994). In addition, these particular group members reside in supportive living situations. It has been suggested elsewhere (Gasker, 1991) that such persons may have training and expectations related to communicating with staff and others but little experience communicating with peers. This may have important implications in the group setting. In addition, they appear to function very highly given their emotional and intellectual limitations. This may be due to the ongoing professional support they receive through their residential programming. They have come to trust paraprofessional and professional staff persons and may be unusual among the population of survivors for that reason. Although the careful description of the entire gestalt is intended to allow the consumer of the research to determine which aspects are generalizable and which are not, the potential for misinterpretation is present.

In addition, this group was unusually small. While the concerns about the legal ramifications of the false memory syndrome debate are likely to be faced by many group facilitators, other groups may continue to be of more traditional size. Perhaps the flavor of interactions within this group is qualitatively different from that which might be expected to occur in a larger group. More study is needed.

In the presence of these limitations, however, the research provides an example of a heretofore unexplored group treatment evaluation tool. This study utilizes a method that permits the use of ethnographic techniques as well as the numerical analysis of quantified variables. In this way, the intimacy that may have been generated by a longer contact with participants has been sacrificed here in favor of a closer look at the moment-to-moment interaction of group members than is possible with traditional ethnographic methods alone. Because the nearly insurmountable access problems reported here are likely to be an ongoing problem for many researchers, it is important to note that many of the access difficulties will be overcome if researchers are willing to study their own practice. Since this study provides some foundation information about the impact of the facilitator on the group process, it will be fruitful for workers to systematically evaluate their own group practices in this manner.

Human Subjects Considerations

The group facilitator's study of his or her own practice may be desirable for reasons other than access. Trust issues have been seen here to be paramount for persons who define themselves as survivors of childhood sexual abuse. Likewise, in light of the current controversy regarding delayed memory recovery, practitioners have also been found to be unlikely to trust researchers. Self-study of one's own practice may be the only acceptable alternative. In this manner, group members may be more comfortable with confidentiality assurances, a consideration that must be made with this population. Simply because a service recipient agrees to participate in a research endeavor does not ensure that he or she is without anxiety regarding the process; concerns of individual study participants should come before research goals at all times. Other precautions that were taken here and that have been recommended by the International Society for Traumatic Stress Studies include the input of human subjects committees into the research design process and the availability of an on-call therapist for the duration of the study (Williams et al., 1994).

One additional advantage to studying one's own practice is the blending of the therapist-researcher role. As a participant observer, I found it impossible to completely divorce myself as researcher from myself as therapist. Although I was able to interview participants relatively objectively most of the time, there were times when it was not possible. For example, the group facilitator asked on several occasions for my input as an experienced clinical supervisor of group therapists. Ethically, I felt I had to respond with honesty, such as when I told her I thought the participants might want to discuss their abuse experiences again. Other times, the needs of the clients had to prevail. For example, when conducting the follow-up interview with Catherine, she stated without a doubt that she felt responsible for the abuse experience she had described for the first time in the group. I felt compelled to ask her whether she had not said she was twelve years old at the time and to point out that I found it hard to believe that a twelve-year-old would be responsible in an interaction with an adult. While the study of one's own work raises unique research biases, such moment-to-moment ethical decisions could be avoided.

Heuristics

It is hoped that this study will encourage more practice-based research of this type. Specific to current concerns about adult recollections of childhood abuse, the results of this study could mark a departure from the narrow focus of research and public concern that has characterized the topic to date. In addition, treatment for survivors of abuse events and re-collections could be improved based on empirical evidence. In general, practice could be systematically and empirically evaluated through the use of this methodology without compromising the perspective of the agency, the therapist, or the client. This type of research could be used to buttress the perceived credibility of the profession as well as providing a response to accountability requirements tied to funding sources.

For group work, the practice implications of this type of research are potentially invaluable. It is clear that the group social process is immensely powerful. As group workers attempt to control that process to enhance the growth of group participants, the knowledge generated by this type of research could well mean the difference between generating the type of group "psychological neighborhood" that is an asylum in its truest sense—a quiet place of safety and healing—and that type of group which is a dysfunctional madhouse.

References

American Psychiatric Association. (1994). *Diagnostic and statistical manual of mental disorders* (Fourth edition). (1994). Washington, DC: American Psychiatric Association.

Bartlett, F.C. (1932). *Remembering: A study in experimental and social psychology.* London: Cambridge University Press.

Berger, P. and Luckmann, T. (1967). *The social construction of reality: A treatise in the sociology of knowledge.* New York: Anchor Books.

Berliner, L. (1993). Treatment of sexual abuse survivors. Paper presented at False Memory Syndrome Foundation Conference, Valley Forge, PA. April 16.

Borgotta, E., Fanshel, D., and Meyer, H. (1960). *Social workers' perceptions of clients.* New York: Russell Sage Foundation.

Bremner, R. (Ed.) (1971). *Children and youth in America: A documentary history.* Cambridge, MA: Harvard University Press.

Brom, D., Kleber, R., and Witzum, E. (1992). The prevalence of post-traumatic psychopathology in the general and the clinical population. *Journal of Psychiatry-Related Science, 28*(4), 53-63.

Bruner, J. (1986). *Actual minds, possible worlds.* Cambridge, MA: Harvard University Press.

Bruner, J. (1990). *Acts of meaning.* Cambridge, MA: Harvard University Press.

Burgess, A. and Hartman, C. (1988). Information processing of trauma: Case application of a model. *Journal of Interpersonal Violence, 3,* 443-457.

Classen, C., Koopman, C., and Spiegel, D. (1993). Trauma and dissociation. *Bulletin of the Menninger Clinic, 57,* 178-194.

Costin, L. (1985). The historical context of child welfare. In J. Laird and A. Hartman (Eds.), *A handbook of child welfare: Context, knowledge and practice* (pp. 154-175). New York: The Free Press.

Davies, J.M. and Frawley, M.G. (1994). *Treating the adult survivor of childhood sexual abuse: A psychoanalytic perspective.* New York: Basic Books.

Dayton, T. (1990). *Drama games: Techniques for self development.* Deerfield Beach, FL: Health Communications.

Denzin, N. (1989). *Interpretive interactionism.* Newbury Park, CA: Sage.

DeShazer, S. (1994). *Words were originally magic.* New York: W.W. Norton.

Devore, W. and Schlesinger, E. G. (1991). *Ethnic-sensitive social work practice* (Third edition). New York: Macmillan.

Donaldson, M.A. and Cordes-Green, S. (1994). *Group treatment of adult incest survivors.* Thousand Oaks, CA: Sage.

Erickson, F. (1992a). Ethnographic microanalysis of interaction. In M. LaCompte, J. Pricell, and W. Melroy (Eds.), *The handbook of qualitative research in education* (pp. 201-225). New York: Academic Press.

Erickson, F. (1992b). They know all the lines: Rhythmic organization and contextualization in a conversational listening routine. In P. Auer and A. Luzio, (Eds.), *The contextualization of language* (pp. 365-397). Philadelphia: John Benjamins.

Fanshel, D. and Moss, F. (1971). *Playback: A marriage in jeopardy examined.* New York: Columbia University Press.

Ferrara, K. W. (1994). *Therapeutic ways with words.* New York: Oxford University Press.

Finkelhor, D., Hotaling, G., Lewis, I.A., and Smith, C. (1990). Sexual abuse in a national survey of adult men and women: Prevalence, characteristics, and risk factors. *Child Abuse and Neglect, 14,* 19-28.

Fisher, S. and Greenberg, R. (1985). *The scientific credibility of Freud's theories and therapy.* New York: Columbia University Press.

Fogel, A. (1993). *Developing through relationships.* Chicago: University of Chicago Press.

Freud, S. (1938). Childhood and concealing memories. In A.A. Brill (Ed.), *The basic writings of Sigmund Freud* (pp. 62-68). New York: The Modern Library.

Freyd, J. (1993). Theoretical and personal perspectives on the delayed memory debate. Paper presented at the Center for Mental Health at Foote Hospital's Continuing Education Conference: Controversies Around Recovered Memories of Incest and Ritualistic Abuse, Ann Arbor, MI. August 23.

Furer, J. (1993). A retractor's story. Oral presentation made at the False Memory Syndrome Foundation Conference, Valley Forge, PA. April 16.

Ganaway, G. (1993). Transference in memory development. Paper presented at False Memory Syndrome Foundation Conference, Valley Forge, PA. April 16.

Gardner, R. (1992a). *Sex abuse hysteria: Salem witch trials revisited.* Cresskill, NJ: Creative Therapeutics.

Gardner, R. (1992b). *True and false accusations of child sexual abuse.* Cresskill, NJ: Creative Therapeutics.

Gasker, J. (1991). Peer communication among adults with mental retardation in a community setting: Patterns and intervention strategies. *Adult Residential Care Journal, 5*(1), 29-43.

Gasker, J. (1993). Beyond the false memory debate: Acquired memories of childhood sexual abuse. Unpublished manuscript, University of Pennsylvania, Philadelphia.

Gasker, J. and Tebb, S. (1995). A residential client's disclosure of incest: An ethnographic microanalysis. *Adult Residential Care Journal, 9*(2), 80-90.

Gavigan-Reno, M. (1993). A retractor's story. Oral presentation made at the False Memory Syndrome Foundation Conference, Valley Forge, PA. April 16.

Germain, C. (1990). Life forces and the anatomy of practice. *Smith College Studies in Social Work, 60,* 547-551.

Goldstein, E. and Farmer, K. (1992). *Confabulations: Creating false memories, destroying families.* Boca Raton, FL: Social Issues Resources Series.

Goldstein, E. and Farmer, K. (1993). *True stories of false memories.* Boca Raton, FL: Social Issues Resources Series.

Hall, E.T. (1981). *Beyond culture.* New York: Anchor-Doubleday.

Hankiss, A. (1981). Ontologies of the self: On the mythological rearranging of one's life history. In D. Bertaux (Ed.), *Biography and society: The life history approach in the social sciences* (pp. 203-209). Beverly Hills, CA: Sage.

Haugaard, J. and Reppucci, N. D. (1988). *The sexual abuse of children.* San Francisco: Jossey-Bass.

Hedges, L.E. (1994). *Remembering, repeating, and working through childhood trauma: The psychodynamics of recovered memories, multiple personality, ritual abuse, incest, molest, and abduction.* Northvale, NJ: Aronson.

Herman, J.L. (1992). *Trauma and recovery: The aftermath of violence—From domestic abuse to political terror.* New York: Basic Books.

Herman, J. and Lawrence, L.R. (1994). Group therapy and self-help groups for adult survivors of childhood incest. In M.B. Williams and J.F. Sommer (Eds.), *Handbook of post-traumatic therapy* (pp. 440-453). Westport, CT: Greenwood Press.

Howing, P. and Wodarski, J. (1992). Legal requisites for social workers in child abuse and neglect situations. *Social Work, 37,* 330-336.

Hufford, D. (1982). *The terror that comes in the night: An experience-centered study of supernatural assault traditions.* Philadelphia: University of Pennsylvania Press.

Hufford, D. (1993). Beings without bodies. Unpublished manuscript, University of Pennsylvania, Philadelphia.

Hunter, M. E. (1994). *Creative scripts for hypnotherapy.* New York: Brunner/Mazel.

Hutchison, E. (1993). Mandatory reporting laws: Child protective case finding gone awry? *Social Work, 38*(1), 56-63.

Janet, P. (1907). *The major symptoms of hysteria.* New York: Hafner Publishing.

Jehu, D., Klassen, C., and Gazan, M. (1985). Cognitive restructuring of distorted beliefs associated with childhood sexual abuse. *Journal of Social Work and Human Sexuality, 4*(1), 49-69.

Kendon, A. (1990). *Conducting interaction: Patterns of behavior in focused encounters.* New York: Cambridge University Press.

Kluft, R. (1992). The use of hypnosis with dissociative disorders. *Psychiatric Medicine, 10*(4), 31-46.

Labov, W. and Fanshel, D. (1977). *Therapeutic discourse: Psychotherapy as conversation.* New York: Academic Press.

Laird, J. (1989). Women and stories: Restorying women's self-constructions. In M. McGoldrick, F. Walsh, and C.M. Anderson (Eds.), *Women in families* (pp. 420-450). New York: Norton.

Lawrence, L. (1993). Backlash: A look at the abuse-related amnesia and delayed memory controversy. *Moving Forward: A Newsjournal for Survivors of Sexual Child Abuse and Those Who Care for Them, 2*(4), 1.

Leudar, I. (1989). Communicative environments for mentally handicapped people. In M. Beveridge, G. Conti-Ramsden, and I. Leudar (Eds.), *Language and communication in mentally handicapped people* (pp. 275-299). New York: Chapman and Hall.

Lief, H. (1992). Psychiatry's challenge: Defining an appropriate therapeutic role when child abuse is suspected. *Psychiatric News*, August 21, 1.

Loftus, E. (1993). Memory distortion. Paper presented at the False Memory Syndrome Foundation Conference, Valley Forge, PA. April 16.

Loftus, E. and Davies, G. (1984). Distortions in the memory of children. *Journal of Social Issues, 40*(2), 51-67.

Loftus, E. and Fathi, D. (1985). Retrieving multiple autobiographical memories. *Social Cognition, 3*, 280-295.

Loftus, E. and Greene, E. (1980). Warning: Even memory for faces may be contagious. *Law and Human Behavior, 4*, 323-334.

Loftus, E. and Loftus, G. (1980). On the permanence of stored information in the human brain. *American Psychologist, 35*, 409-420.

Lynn, S.J. and Rhue, J.W. (Eds.) (1994). *Dissociation: Clinical and theoretical perspectives.* New York: The Guilford Press.

Maltz, W. (1990). Adult survivors of incest: How to help them overcome the trauma. *Medical Aspects of Human Sexuality, 12*, 42-47.

Maltz, W. and Holman, B. (1987). *Incest and sexuality: A guide to understanding and healing.* Lexington, MA: Lexington Books.

Masson, J. (1984). *The assault on truth.* New York: Penguin Books.

McAdams, D.P. (1993). *The stories we live by.* New York: William Morrow.

McDougall, J. (1985). *Theatres of the mind: Illusion and truth on the psychoanalytic stage.* Basic Books: New York.

Miller, A. (1983). *For your own good: Hidden cruelty in child-rearing and the roots of violence.* New York: The Noonday Press.

Morales, A. and Sheafor, B. W. (1998). *Social work: A profession of many faces* (Seventh edition). Needham, MA: Allyn and Bacon.

Newman, K. (1990). Harry Stack Sullivan. In H. A. Bacal and K. M. Newman (Eds.), *Theories of object relations: Bridges to self psychology* (pp. 28-52). New York: Columbia University Press.

Palmer, L.M. (Ed.) (1988). *On the most ancient wisdom of the Italians.* Ithaca, NY: Cornell University Press.

Parry, A. and Doan, R.E. (1994). *Story revisions: Narrative therapy in the post-modern world.* New York: Guilford.

Perry, C. (1993). Hypnotic enhancement of memory. Paper presented at the False Memory Syndrome Foundation Conference, Valley Forge, PA. April 16.

Peters, S.D. (1988). Child sexual abuse and later psychological problems. In G.E. Wyatt and G. J. Powell (Eds.), *Lasting effects of child sexual abuse* (pp. 101-117). Newbury Park, CA: Sage.

Phelps, A., Friedlander, M. L., and Enns, C. Z. (1997). Psychotherapy process variables associated with the retrieval of memories of childhood sexual abuse: A qualitative study. *Journal of Counseling Psychology, 44*(3), 321-332.

Reissman, C. (1989). From victim to survivor: A woman's narrative reconstruction of marital sexual abuse. *Smith College Studies in Social Work, 59*, 232-251.

Robinson, J.A. and Hawpe, L. (1994). Narrative thinking as a heuristic process. In T.R. Sarbin (Ed.), *Narrative psychology: The storied nature of human conduct* (pp. 111-128). New York: Praeger.

Saleebey, D. (1994). Culture, theory, and narrative: The intersection of meanings in practice. *Social Work, 39*(4), 351-359.

Sands, R.G. (1988). Sociolinguistic analysis of a mental health interview. *Social Work, 33*(2), 149-154.

Sands, R.G. (1996). The elusiveness of identity in social work practice with women: A postmodern feminist perspective. *Clinical Social Work Journal, 24*(2), 167-186.

Schafer, R. (1976). *A new language for psychoanalysis.* New Haven, CT: Yale University Press.

Schafer, R. (1992). *Retelling a life: Narration and dialogue in psychoanalysis.* New York: Basic Books.

Scheflen, A. (1973). *Communicational structure: Analysis of a psychotherapy transaction.* Bloomington, IN: Indiana University Press.

Schlegoff, E.A., Jefferson, G., and Sacks, H. (1977). The preference for self-correction in the organization of repair in conversation. *Language, 53*(2), 361-382.

Schlegoff, E. and Sacks, H. (1974). Opening up closings. In R. Turner (Ed.), *Ethnomethodology* (pp. 233-264). Middlesex, England: Penguin Education

Schneider, W. and Pressley, M. (1989). *Memory development between 2 and 20.* New York: Springer-Verlag.

Schwartz, W. (1969). Private troubles and public issues: One social work job or two? In W. Schwartz (Ed.), *National conference on social welfare: The social welfare forum* (pp. 22-43). New York: Columbia University Press.

Simonds, S. L. (1994). *Bridging the silence: Nonverbal modalities in the treatment of adult survivors of childhood sexual abuse.* New York: W.W. Norton.

Singer, J.A. and Salovey, P. (1993). *The remembered self: Emotion and memory in personality.* New York: The Free Press.

Smalley, R. (1967). *Theory for social work practice.* New York: Columbia University Press.

Spence, D. (1982). *Narrative truth and historical truth: Meaning and interpretation in psychoanalysis.* New York: W.W. Norton.

Spence, D. (1994). Narrative smoothing and clinical wisdom. In T.R. Sarbin (Ed.), *Narrative psychology: The storied nature of human conduct* (pp. 211-232). New York: Praeger.

Spiegel, D. (1990). Hypnosis, dissociation, and trauma. In J. L. Singer (Ed.), *Repression and dissociation: Implications for personality theory, psychopathology, and health* (pp. 121-142). Chicago: University of Chicago Press.

Tavris, C. (1993). Beware the incest-survivor machine. *The New York Times*, January 3, section 7, 1:1. Reprinted in *False Memory Syndrome Foundation Newsletter*, pp. 13-15. January 8.

Tillman, J.G., Nash, M.R., and Lerner, P.M. (1996). Does trauma cause dissociative pathology? In S.J. Lynn (Ed.), *Dissociation: Clinical, theoretical and research perspectives* (pp. 90-109). Washington, DC: American Psychological Press.

Van der Kolk, B. and Van der Hart, O. (1991). The intrusive past: The flexibility of memory and the engraving of trauma. *American Imago, 48*, 425-454.

Victors, J. (1993). *Satanic panic: The creation of a contemporary legend.* Chicago: Open Court.

Waites, E.A. (1997). *Memory quest: Trauma and the search for personal history.* New York: W.W. Norton.

Wakefield, H. and Underwager, R. (1988). *Accusations of child sexual abuse.* Springfield, IL: Charles Thomas.

Williams, M.B. (1994). Establishing safety in survivors of severe sexual abuse. In M.B. Williams and J.F. Sommer (Eds.), *Handbook of post-traumatic therapy* (pp. 163-178). Westport, CT: Greenwood Press.

Williams, M.B., Sommer, J.F., Stamm, B.H., and Harris, C.J. (1994). Ethical considerations in trauma treatment, research, publication, and training. In M.B. Williams and J.F. Sommer (Eds.), *Handbook of post-traumatic therapy* (pp. 521-539). Westport, CT: Greenwood Press.

Young, L. (1992). Sexual abuse and the problem of embodiment. *Child Abuse and Neglect, 16*(1), 89-100.

Zelizer, V. (1985). *Pricing the priceless child: The changing social value of children.* New York: Basic Books.

Index

Page numbers followed by the letter "f" indicate figures; those followed by the letter "t" indicate tables.

Order Your Own Copy of
This Important Book for Your Personal Library!

"I NEVER TOLD ANYONE THIS BEFORE"
Managing the Initial Disclosure of Sexual Abuse Re-Collections

_____ in hardbound at $29.95 (ISBN: 0–7890-0461-5)

_____ in softbound at $39.95 (ISBN: 0-7890-0462-3)

COST OF BOOKS_____

OUTSIDE USA/CANADA/
MEXICO: ADD 20%_____

POSTAGE & HANDLING_____
(US: $3.00 for first book & $1.25
for each additional book)
Outside US: $4.75 for first book
& $1.75 for each additional book)

SUBTOTAL_____

IN CANADA: ADD 7% GST_____

STATE TAX_____
(NY, OH & MN residents, please
add appropriate local sales tax)

FINAL TOTAL_____
(If paying in Canadian funds,
convert using the current
exchange rate. UNESCO
coupons welcome.)

☐ **BILL ME LATER:** ($5 service charge will be added)
(Bill-me option is good on US/Canada/Mexico orders only;
not good to jobbers, wholesalers, or subscription agencies.)

☐ Check here if billing address is different from
shipping address and attach purchase order and
billing address information.

Signature_____

☐ **PAYMENT ENCLOSED: $**_____

☐ **PLEASE CHARGE TO MY CREDIT CARD.**

☐ Visa ☐ MasterCard ☐ AmEx ☐ Discover
☐ Diner's Club

Account #_____

Exp. Date_____

Signature_____

Prices in US dollars and subject to change without notice.

NAME _____

INSTITUTION _____

ADDRESS _____

CITY _____

STATE/ZIP _____

COUNTRY _____ COUNTY (NY residents only) _____

TEL _____ FAX _____

E-MAIL_____
May we use your e-mail address for confirmations and other types of information? ☐ Yes ☐ No

Order From Your Local Bookstore or Directly From
The Haworth Press, Inc.
10 Alice Street, Binghamton, New York 13904-1580 • USA
TELEPHONE: 1-800-HAWORTH (1-800-429-6784) / Outside US/Canada: (607) 722-5857
FAX: 1-800-895-0582 / Outside US/Canada: (607) 772-6362
E-mail: getinfo@haworthpressinc.com
PLEASE PHOTOCOPY THIS FORM FOR YOUR PERSONAL USE.

BOF96